The History, Ecology and Archaeology of Medieval Parks and Parklands

Landscape Archaeology and Ecology, Volume 6, 2007

Front Cover Picture - © Ian D. Rotherham

Edited by Ian D. Rotherham

ISSN 1354-0262
ISBN 1-904098-03-7

Printed by: B&B Press (Parkgate) Rotherham

Published by: Wildtrack Publishing, P.O. Box 1142, Sheffield, S1 1SZ

Typeset and processed by: Diane Harrison and Christine Handley

Supported by: Biodiversity and Landscape History Research Institute, Hallam Environmental Consultants Ltd, Tourism Leisure and Environmental Change Research Unit at Sheffield Hallam University.

Medieval Parks and Parklands: a Preamble and Introduction

Ian D. Rotherham
Sheffield Hallam University

Medieval parks have been the subject of research and debate for many decades, but until relatively recently have remained neglected in terms of their conservation. There is a rich literature, with studies of invertebrate faunas and their ecologies, rare lichens and bryophytes, and grazing stock such as deer and old park cattle. Researchers have considered their fishponds, and other productive features. Political historians and medievalists have written on the politics of fashion and taste and the importance of parks in providing sport and entertainment for the wealthy elite. There are also regional studies that document parks in their county or national contexts, and individual case studies that look in depth at particular locations. A major area of research is the study of old trees in parks and also of the need today, to manage these effectively. Yet it is only by understanding the economic and political forces that generated and safeguarded these magnificent trees and their landscapes, alongside the unique ecological interest for example, that we can fully engage with them. It is only then that we can most effectively find ways in which to both celebrate their histories, and seek to conserve them for the future. Many of these topics are covered by the papers in this volume.

It is clear that parks present opportunities for in-depth, multi-disciplinary research. However, it is also apparent that much more could be done in this respect. The conference at Sheffield Hallam University in September 2007 will hopefully be a catalyst for further co-operation. It is only through such collaborations that the complex nature and variety of medieval park landscapes can be most fully appreciated. However, with each specialist area of interest and expertise having its own meetings and publishing it's own literature, many opportunities are lost. The work of each discipline is excellent in its own sphere, but they cry out for a coming together and a synergy of shared efforts. There is also the issue that many relevant areas of interest are covered by work on areas other than parks. Aspects of forests and chases, their history and ecology, are also pertinent to an understanding of parklands. In many cases, there is an intimate if changing relationship between parks, forest and other unenclosed landscapes. Parklands, steeped in history and driven by economy and politics, have evolved uniquely rich ecologies and fascinating heritage interest. It is important to understand and appreciate the wildlife and heritage of medieval parks in the context of not only their ecology, but of the social factors that underpin their origins and survival. Their academic study of medieval parkland therefore crosses with that of recreation, of hunting, and of productive landscapes (chases, forests, wooded commons, and wastes). There is a rich vein of literature on hunting, on deer and on associated activities such as falconry. Food production literature includes that on warrens and fishponds

The dead and dying wood of historic parks provides unique opportunities for specialist biodiversity: fungi, invertebrates, slime moulds, with birds such as woodpeckers, and owls benefiting, along with bats, from ancient trees. Indeed it is the veteran trees and their dead wood that nature conservationists see as the priority resource. There are even EU regulations that target dead wood because of its diverse associated faunas and floras. Habitat loss and degradation have led to critical declines across Europe. Finding, preserving, and conserving this heritage is a major challenge with no single approach or correct answer. The work of the *Woodland Trust* and other organisations such as the *Ancient Tree Forum* in involving local people and engaging local communities is surely the way forward. However, to be most effective it is important that this engagement and education reflects the multi-disciplinary nature of these wonderful landscapes. If we accept that at least in part, these remnants of medieval parks are vestiges of more ancient landscapes transformed by human hand over centuries, but with a lineage to primeval origins of the European forest and savannah, then the story is even more important. These landscapes evoke a rich past but they also throw out a challenge to our future visions of the environment. Our deeply embedded precepts of nature conservation may be changed through a new understanding of the now scattered and fragmentary, but once numerous and great, medieval parks. This is a powerful lineage and an exciting future.

Contents

Keith Alexander	Old growth: ageing and decaying processes in trees	8
John Barnatt	Chatsworth: the Parkland Archaeology	13
Lawrence Bee	Conservation of Arachnids in Ancient Trees	18
Jill Butler	Securing a future for our parkland ancient and veteran trees	22
Christopher Dingwall	Deer Parks in Scotland: A Neglected Heritage	25
Joy Ede	Natural England Crusader for the Environment (Poster)	29
John Fletcher	The rise and fall of British deer parks: their raison d'etre in a global and historical perspective.	31
Julian Forbes-Laird	Tree Management in Historic Parks	45
Monica Gillespie	'The living dead - A quantitative study of standing dead wood in three ancient wood pasturesites in Derbyshire' (Poster)	46
Ted Green	Stating the Obvious - From Acorn to Ancient	48
Stephen Hall	Chillingham Wild Cattle Park, Northumberland	53
Peter Hammond & Nigel Reeve	Saproxylic beetle survey of Richmond Park 2005-7 (Poster)	58
Peter Herring	Historic and Archaeological Survey of Cornish Deer Parks	60
Melvyn Jones	Deer Parks in South Yorkshire: The Documentary and Landscape Evidence	65
Roger Key	Chatsworth: Invertebrates and the Veteran Trees	79
Rob Liddiard	The disparkment of medieval deer parks	82
Stephen Mileson	The Social Impact of Park Making in the Middle Ages	83
Stephen Moorhouse	Medieval Parks in Yorkshire: range and context	84
Amanda Richardson	"The King's Chief Delights": Visits to the Royal Deer Parks in the Later Middle Ages	85
Ian Rotherham	The Ecology and Economics of Medieval Deer Parks	86
Naomi Sykes	Animal bones and animal parks	103
David Thackray	The National Trust's Historic Parkland Project	105
Frans Vera	The Park in the Forest Landscape	107
Tom Williamson	Chatsworth: the Parkland History	113
Mary Wiltshire & Sue Woore	Medieval Parks in Duffield Frith and elsewhere in Derbyshire (joint)	114

Old growth: ageing and decaying processes in trees

Keith N A Alexander

Ancient Tree Forum

Introduction

Old growth covers two key aspects of trees and shrubs - their growth, development and decay, on the one hand, and the unique biological communities associated with sites with a long and unbroken history of ageing and decay. Neither has achieved much prominence in biodiversity conservation in the UK, but this does seem to be changing, albeit slowly. The understanding of the processes involved has increased dramatically in recent decades but adoption into mainstream nature conservation continues to be problematic - twentieth century hypotheses and attitudes still dominate conservation thinking and land management practices.

Growth, development and decay in trees and shrubs

Given adequate space and time, most broad-leaved trees develop and age in a very characteristic way. The young tree develops a canopy that optimises its light-gathering potential, with variations in canopy size and shape tending to reflect differences in genetic composition, soil conditions, and climate. A key driving force in the development of the tree is the obligatory development of new annual rings; the trunk girth continues to expand throughout the life of the tree - the exceptions being where parts rip out following structural failure.

Each tree has its own potential maximum canopy development, and this is generally referred to as the mature or full canopy. Canopy development is relatively rapid in the first phase of growth, but slows with maturity. While the mature canopy phase is relatively slow to change, annual rings continue to be laid down and the girths of trunk and boughs continue to expand.

Each new annual ring has a genetically defined life expectancy, which is around 20-30 years in English oak *Quercus robur* (D. Lonsdale, pers. comm.). So, by the time the canopy is maturing, the trunk and main boughs of an oak tree contain a high proportion of dead annual rings within their core, and this core of dead woody tissue is referred to as the heartwood. In some trees, beech *Fagus sylvatica* and ash *Fraxinus excelsior* for example, the death of the inner annual rings is less precisely controlled by age, and there is a middle zone of mixed living and dead tissues between the inner dead rings and the outer young live rings; this situation is referred to as ripewood.

The accumulations of dead woody tissues in the core of tree trunks and boughs provide opportunities for colonisation by wood-decay fungi, particularly bracket fungi. It remains unclear how the fungi find their way in to the central core but one suggestion is through the base of the tree, where the original taproot of the seedling tree is long dead and gone, replaced by networks of lateral roots, but leaving the base of the trunk as exposed dead tissue. The bracket fungi are primarily specialists of heartwood and ripewood, the dead woody tissues deep within the trunk and main boughs, which are broken down from complex carbohydrates into simpler compounds that can be used by a wide range of other organisms. The implications of this central decay and hollowing for the structural integrity of the tree are the subject of considerable debate. Equally, the extent to which some of the bracket fungi are capable of breaking into living woody tissue - and the conditions under which this can occur - is also subject of considerable debate.

This central decay is mainly hidden from view and most people are completely unaware of what is happening within the tree. Only once the outer structure of the trunk or boughs is damaged in some way, by some means, does the decay and hollowing become apparent, and only then can the fungi gain access to the outside for fruiting

Returning to the new annual rings, these are being grown around an ever-increasing circumference each year, and so they tend to become thinner and thinner. Eventually the girth of the tree becomes so great that a complete viable ring is no longer biologically possible, and the ring fragments. Columns of exposed woody tissues begin to appear on the exterior of the trunk, independent of any structural damage.

Also full canopy development cannot be maintained indefinitely, and gradually the tree becomes incapable of providing sufficient water through its vascular system to sustain a full canopy. This can happen in periods of drought when a high canopy bough may be 'dropped' in order to reduce the water demand, summer branch drop. However, at a certain age, branch-death in the canopy becomes the norm, and the high canopy gradually breaks up. As light levels reaching the lower boughs increase so dormant buds respond and reiterative growth forms - a new low canopy is formed, the tree 'grows downwards' (E.E. Green, pers. comm.). The canopy break-up is not the result of failing health, only ageing of the woody structure, the tree biology reaching a stage where it is no longer possible to maintain the high canopy. The new low canopy may be vigorous and productive - the living tissues are all less than 20-30 years old after all, but covering an aged framework. The canopy break-up is referred to as retrenchment and this is the beginning of the ancient phase of the tree's growth.

These aspects of tree biology need to be understood and appreciated, before the importance and implications of old growth to biodiversity conservation can be understood and appreciated.

Old growth - a woodland ecosystem distinct from any younger age class

The starting point of the preceding discussion was 'given adequate space and time'. The life cycle described relates only to open-grown trees (see also Green, 2007). Where trees grow alongside other trees then canopy competition has a significant impact on tree form and life expectancy. The tree form that optimises light gathering under competition is a tall tree with very limited lateral branching. Such a tree cannot develop into an ancient tree if competition from neighbouring trees is maintained, and so, when retrenchment becomes inevitable with age, the retrenching tree is quickly over-shadowed by its neighbours and dies as a result of the reduced light levels. Often the trunk of such top-heavy tall trees snaps in high winds before retrenchment is reached. Ancient trees cannot exist under temperate high forest conditions (G.F. Peterken, pers. comm.).

Yet a great diversity of fungi and invertebrates are wood-decay species (Rayner & Boddy, 1988; Alexander, 2002), and these include a high proportion of species specializing in exploiting canopy retrenchment, lateral branch development, and trunk hollowing. The latter are especially species-rich in sites known to have had long continuity of large old trees and these species are also prominent in sub-fossil deposits dating from the post-glacial forest period (Buckland & Dinnin, 1993; Alexander 1998, 2004, 2005; Alexander & Butler, 2004). Epiphytic communities that are light demanding provide a parallel story. These are most species-rich on open-grown trees, least diverse on high forest trees (Harding & Rose, 1986; Fletcher *et al.*, 2001). Clearly ancient trees have been present and locally prominent since before people started modifying the tree cover that developed following the last Ice Age.

There are currently two main hypotheses on the structure of the post-glacial forest: high forest (the 'Tansley' theory) and savanna, or wood pasture (Vera, 2000). Rackham (2006) includes an interesting and personal discussion of the two alternatives, but is not unbiased. Vascular plant ecologists predominate amongst the Tansley high forest school while more broadly based ecologists tend to favour the Vera model. Both are hypotheses and there is evidence in favour of both - see Rackham's Table 9 for example. However, this high forest model is clearly inadequate since it would appear to predict that organisms associated with trees would be primarily adapted to dense stands and shaded trunks, which is not what our present knowledge indicates. The attraction of the Vera model is that it works for all of the relict old growth species that are known. The true situation may never be confirmed, the distant past is a very foreign country and largely beyond our comprehension, but sub-fossil organic remains offer tantalizing glimpses. It is unfortunate that so far we cannot agree on their interpretation.

Vera proposes that large herbivores are key drivers of forest structure, maintaining dynamic mosaic landscapes of varying tree density. Openness is a strong feature of this new hypothesis and so the Vera landscape is compatible with knowledge of fungi, lichens, and invertebrates, in a way that the high forest hypothesis is not.

A high proportion of wood decay invertebrates and epiphytic lichens are today strongly associated with places with a long history of open-grown trees and with ancient trees. This is no coincidence, as palaeo-ecologists have found evidence for the presence of many of the same beetle species in deposits dated to the postglacial forest period. The beetle *Prostomis mandibularis* is frequent in these deposits and is today known from just a few areas of extensive, landscape-scale, **open**, ancient forest country. It is extinct in Britain, Ireland and across much of northern Europe (Whitehouse, 2006), where fragmentation of habitat and isolation of populations has led to decline and loss. Other species present in these dated deposits do survive in modern Britain and are concentrated in historic parklands and the few remaining old forests that maintain

networks of large old open-grown trees. Most palynologists however steadfastly ignore this evidence.

The web-site of the Convention on Biological Diversity provides a definition of old growth: stands in primary or secondary forests that have developed the structures and species normally associated with old primary woodland of that type that have sufficiently accumulated to act as a woodland ecosystem distinct from any younger age class (Alexander *et al*, 2003). Although difficult to comprehend in total, the various sections of this definition hold much of interest. Old growth can be in primary or secondary forests, and so arguments based on old growth confined to primeval or pristine forest are discarded. Cultural landscapes can hold old growth. As already mentioned, there are two main hypotheses about the structure of old primary woodland, and so we should not consider structure associated with old primary woodland, as we cannot agree on what this was. That leaves the species of old primary woodland, where we have good clues from the dated deposits, and accumulations of these species which distinguish the old growth stands from younger age classes, which neatly brings us to the historic parklands which we know to be rich in old growth species.

The special biological communities of old growth tree populations in historic parklands - when will Cinderella reach her due prominence at the ball?

Historic parklands are where ancient trees are concentrated, and to a far greater extent today than at any previous period of history. These parklands were mostly developed by enclosing areas of old medieval forest and wood pasture, or at least areas with old hedgerow trees - trees were an essential feature of a park and so instant parks were preferable to starting from completely clear land and having to plant. The origin of most parks from ancient forest and wood pasture also captured the old growth fungi, invertebrates, and lichens.

Despite this, nature conservationists in Britain still equate trees with 'woodlands' and fail to grasp the significance of trees in other situations. The inclusion of '*Wood Pasture and Parkland*' as a Priority Habitat under the *UK Biodiversity Action Plan* has raised the profile of non-woodland trees to some extent. However, these still fail to be considered by many landscape ecologists and nature conservation professionals; forest habitat network models continue to fail to see trees as part of the landscape (see Ray *et al.*, 2004, and Latham *et al.*, 2004, for example). The mindset is still that trees belong in concentrations, i.e. 'woods', and are at best irrelevant elsewhere and at worst need to be weeded out, e.g. from heathlands or calcareous grasslands. Manning et al. (2006) are amongst the few international ecologists to realize the true significance of trees and shrubs outside of 'woods'.

Historic parklands are part of our special national heritage and combine special wildlife, history, and landscape features; they merit far greater prominence in conservation and demand a uniquely integrated land management approach.

Acknowledgements

The formation of the Ancient Tree Forum has transformed knowledge of the conservation significance of ancient trees and shrubs, and this paper draws heavily on knowledge shared amongst the membership and supporters. I would particularly like to acknowledge discussions with Ted Green, Jill Butler, Francis Rose, Nev Fay, David Lonsdale, and Vikki Forbes.

References

Alexander, K.N.A. (1998) *The links between forest history and biodiversity: the invertebrate fauna of ancient pasture-woodlands in Britain and its conservation*. In: Kirby, K.J., & Watkins, C. (Eds.) The Ecological History of European Forests. CABI, Hungerford pp 73-80

Alexander, K.N.A. (2002) The invertebrates of living and decaying timber in Britain and Ireland - a provisional annotated checklist. *English Nature Research Reports*, No. **467**

Alexander, K.N.A. (2004) *Landscapes with ancient trees: invertebrate mobility and population viability*. In: Smithers, R. (Ed.) *Landscape Ecology of Trees and Forests*. IALE (UK). pp107-114

Alexander, K.N.A. (2005) Wood decay, insects, palaeoecology, and woodland conservation policy and practice - breaking the halter. *Antenna*, **29**, (3), 171-178

Alexander, K.N.A. & Butler, J.E. (2004) *Is the US Concept of 'Old Growth' relevant to the cultural landscapes of Europe? A UK perspective*. In: Honnay, O., Verheyen, K., Bossuyt, B., & Hermy, M. (Eds.) *Forest Biodiversity: Lessons from History for Conservation*. CABI, Hungerford pp 233-246

Alexander, K., Smith, M., Stiven, R., & Sanderson, N. (2003) Defining 'old growth' in the UK context. *English Nature Research Reports*, **No 494**

Buckland, P.C., & Dinnin, M.H. (1993) Holocene woodlands, the fossil insect evidence. In: Kirby, K.J., & Drake, C.M. (Eds.) Dead wood matters: the ecology and conservation of saproxylic invertebrates in Britain. *English Nature Science*, **No. 7**. pp 6-20

Fletcher, A., Wolseley, P. & Woods, R. (Eds.) (2001) *Lichen Habitat Management*. British Lichen Society & Countryside Council for Wales, British Lichen Society.

Green, E.E. (2007) Stating the obvious - the biodiversity of open grown trees - from acorn to ancient. (Proceedings of this conference).

Harding, P.T. & Rose, F. (1986) *Pasture-woodlands in lowland Britain*. ITE, Monks Wood Experimental Station, Huntingdon

Latham, J., Watts, K., Thomas, C. & Griffiths, M. (2004) *Development of a forest habitat network for Wales: linking research with policy*. In: Smithers, R. (Ed.) Landscape Ecology of Trees and Forests. IALE (UK). pp 224-231

Manning, A.D., Fischer, J. & Lindenmayer, D.B. (2006) Scattered trees are keystone structures - implications for conservation. *Biological Conservation*, **132**, 311-321

Rackham, O. (2006) *Woodlands*. Collins New Naturalist, 100, Collins, London.

Ray, D., Watts, K., Hope, J. & Humphrey, J. (2004) *Developing forest habitat networks in southern Scotland*. In: Smithers, R. (Ed.) *Landscape Ecology of Trees and Forests*. IALE (UK). pp 216-223

Rayner, A.D.M. & Boddy, L. (1988) *Fungal decomposition of wood: its biology and ecology*. John Wiley & Sons, London

Vera, F.W.M. (2000) *Grazing Ecology and Forest History*. CABI, Hungerford

Whitehouse, N.J. (2006) The Holocene British and Irish ancient forest fossil beetle fauna: implications for forest history, biodiversity and faunal colonization. *Quaternary Science Reviews*, **25 (15)**, 1755-1789

Chatsworth: the parkland archaeology

John Barnatt
Peak National Park

Abstract

Many thousands of people visit Chatsworth every year, but how many realise that there is an exceptional wealth of archaeological features in the landscape park designed for the fourth Duke of Devonshire by Lancelot 'Capability' Brown from 1759 into the 1760s? Many speed past on their way to the House and its gardens, while even those who walk in the park need a keen eye to spot many of the clues to past land-uses. About 250 archaeological sites have been recorded, many identified for the first time during systematic field assessment by the author in 1995-96. These features, often low earthworks, extend over much of the parkland. Over large parts, sometimes the whole land surface is one continuous archaeological carpet. This one of the true wonders of Chatsworth. Many of these earthworks present a 'fossilised' agricultural landscape of about 1760 when the core part of the park was created, or elsewhere when it was enlarged in the 1820s. A few features have survived from prehistoric times, far more date from the era when medieval open fields were the norm or from the eighteenth and nineteenth centuries when the valley was covered in hedged fields. There is also evidence for radical changes to the designed landscape and the routeways that pass through this, which have taken place since the park was first laid out.

From 1995 to 2000, detailed surveys and archive reports were carried out for the whole of the Chatsworth Core Estate. These were followed in 2002 by a detailed interpretative archive report describing the historic landscape. The archaeological assessment was carried out by this author, complemented by building, woodland and field boundary surveys carried out by Nicola Bannister, all commissioned by the Trustees of the Chatsworth Settlement and

English Heritage. This work was complemented by a separate assessment of the designed landscape. The first published output has been an account of the designed and archaeological landscapes of Chatsworth's park and gardens, published in 2005 by John Barnatt and Tom Williamson. This is to be followed by an overview of the archaeology of the whole of the Chatsworth Core Estate by John Barnatt and Nicola Bannister, which is in preparation.

The conference paper by Tom Williamson introduces Chatsworth House, the home of the Cavendish family from the mid-sixteenth century. It discusses the history of Chatsworth's park in some detail. In contrast, the second Chatsworth paper by me, on the archaeology of the parkland, gives a virtual tour of the park introducing the wide variety of features of different dates found cheek-by-jowl wherever you walk. This set the scene for the Sheffield 2007 Conference site visit to Chatsworth when some of the features mentioned were encountered.

The archaeology recorded in the landscape park includes a wide variety of historic features of different types, created over a broad range of dates, which add much to our understanding of the Chatsworth landscape. Amongst the highlights brought into focus by the archaeological survey are the extensive but low earthworks of removed field boundaries, their lines 'fossilised' when the landscape park was created. There are many hectares of ridge and furrow, much of which has medieval origins. In many instances, mature oaks and other trees that once stood in hedgerows were retained as ornamental features within the park and some still stand today. Other even older oaks north and south of the house grew within a medieval deer park before Brown's landscape parkland was created. Amongst the many remains of the medieval and post-medieval farmed landscape, there are older features, including two if not three newly discovered prehistoric barrows, their identification at a stroke doubling the number of known examples in the Derwent Valley. North of the House, there are important earthworks around Queen Mary's Bower, of extensive ornamental gardens with sixteenth century origins that were subsequently swept away, bearing witness to the changing fashions in garden layouts around our stately homes.

In the virtual tour through the Chatsworth Park, I concentrate not on the familiar, such as the architect designed lodges, bridges, mill and stables, but on lesser known and often subtle earthworks and what they tell us about life around Chatsworth before and after the creation of the grand house and all that went with it. Some features take us back 4,000 years! There is not enough space to even mention all that exists, but only pick out selected highlights. In contrast with what is to be found at the house and gardens, the archaeological features are often un-photogenic, other than under exceptional circumstances, as under light snow when even earthworks such as the ridge and furrow suddenly become more visible. It is often only when all low features in an area are carefully plotted and looked at together that their meaning becomes clear.

The tour starts north of the house, close to where visitors normally park their cars. Surrounding Queen Mary's Bower, a small walled garden surrounded by a shallow oval pond, there is a rare survival of geometrically arranged earthworks that are all that remain, in modified form, of Chatsworth's sixteenth century formal gardens to the north of the house. Here there were once six large ornamental fishponds, together with orchards, linked by a grid of paths. While much of this was swept away for Brown in the 1760s, one small area, partially hidden by trees and called the Rookery Gardens, survived into the 1820s. However, this was dismantled at around the time the Bower itself was restored by the architect Wyatville, leaving only the earthworks we see today.

Nearby, a relatively small area of the parkland east of the Bower is atypical in that it is devoid of archaeological features; the site of a seventeenth century ornamental canal that was infilled for Brown. It was similar in size to that south of the House where the nineteenth century Emperor Fountain still jets water high into the air. There are local traditions of vast earthmoving undertaken for Brown. However, earlier earthworks throughout the rest of the park show unequivocally that the only radical landforming that took place here was near the Bower and at an even smaller area west of the house where the river was widened to make it lake-like.

Running along the slopes going north from the House there are a number of veteran oaks that date back to late medieval times and once stood within the old deer park. This park, the predecessor of the landscape park, extended up the scarp slope to the Stand (a sixteenth century hunting tower), and across the broad shelf beyond. At this time, the land later transformed by Brown was largely agricultural in character. The veterans lie in the narrow zone where the two parks overlapped. Many of these trees were once pollarded, while others were shredded for deer fodder. In the private part of the park south of the House, there are many equally old oaks whose survival is explained by similar practices. Some of these are growing on what had formerly been medieval cultivation strips in use before the deer park was created. The local tradition that the Chatsworth oaks were once part of Sherwood Forest is not true.

Much of the north-eastern parkland has denuded field-boundary hedge-banks. When mapped, these low features show the pre-park agricultural layout. Close to the house this was swept away in about 1760. Going further north, beyond the eighteenth century walled kitchen gardens to as far as the Golden Gates, there were fields still in existence until the 1820s when the park was radically enlarged. Here there are the foundations of a seventeenth or eighteenth century farmstead or small hamlet. Many trees across this part of the park started life standing in the hedgerows. When these boundaries were removed selected trees were retained to help create the desired 'instant' parkland landscape with trees scattered tastefully throughout. Within some of the fields, both here and south of the House, there is broad medieval-type ridge and furrow, together with strip lynchets, some probably unploughed since the small medieval farming settlements of Chatsworth, Langley and Besley were abandoned. Other examples of ploughing earthworks may well be later, some perhaps last cultivated in the early nineteenth century.

When the park was created in around 1760, functional features such as the northern icehouse were made. This largely buried building has a small but deep reservoir pond above. In winter, water was run from here into a shallow ice pond below. The ice that was formed overnight was cut and stored in the icehouse until needed at the house for refrigeration. Other eighteenth century features in this part of the park have now gone, removed to leave only slight traces, such as a lodge on the then main drive that ran just above the icehouse, and a deer house on the slopes above.

Beyond the original landscape park and its lodge at the northern boundary, within farmland to the north owned by the Duke of Rutland until the 1820s, there ran the 1759 turnpike road from Baslow to Chesterfield. This can still be traced as a low straight terrace, the road itself having been moved northwards to beyond tree screens at the edge of new 1820s park when this was created. High on the parkland's eastern slopes there is the deep sinuous hollow way of the medieval road that the turnpike road replaced. Close by on Dobb Edge, hidden by trees, there are old millstone quarries, with broken, and unfinished domed-millstones still lying where abandoned. These were probably mostly created in the seventeenth or eighteenth century, although millstones have been made around Baslow since medieval times. The overgrown quarries hidden in this obscure part of the park provide a reminder of the traditional importance of industrial endeavours in the Peak District landscape, which commonly included lead, copper and coal mining, quarrying, lime burning, charcoal production and metal smelting. Few people today realise that

extensive industrial wastelands once existed across the National Park; the scars have largely healed. Ironically, industrial exploitation at mines and other industrial sites across the Peak and beyond, and the transformations of the countryside this entailed, helped the Dukes of Devonshire finance the creation and maintenance of the idealised parkland landscape around Chatsworth.

Turning now to the parkland on the west side of the Derwent. At the edge is the model village of Edensor, what is visible today largely created in the late-1830s and early-1840s. Contrary to common opinion, the old village of Edensor was not demolished and moved by the sixth Duke because it was visible from the house. Rather one half was demolished in the late-1810s to early-1830s to create an unobstructed carriage route to the house; this part of the village was never visible from the house. In the mid-1830s, a new plan by the Duke and Paxton evolved; the western part of the village was restructured in an eclectic mixture of architectural styles as a showpiece, although one that was masked behind a screen of trees until late in the nineteenth century. Some of the village houses were newly built, while others were older but refaced.

Until the late 1750s, a large part of the slopes running up from the river north of Edensor was used as a rabbit warren, which was probably created in late medieval times. This provided food and furs for the family. Rabbits, along with deer, were exotic foods and commonly reared on grand estates as status symbols at that time. For much of its life the Chatsworth warren was a large grass-covered open-sward only bounded at its edge, with a warrener's lodge at the centre. There were small oval mounds made especially for the rabbits to inhabit, some of which are visible today as low earthworks known to archaeologists as pillow mounds. In the first half of the eighteenth century the open grassland of the warren was transformed by subdividing it into a series of hedged fields, the banks of which still survive. The area was rented out for the grazing of stock and the internal fields no doubt helped their management, but large numbers of rabbits continued to be reared until 1758.

The warren area also has medieval open field earthworks dating from an earlier period, when this land was cultivated by the villagers of Edensor. Nearby, there are prominent strip lynchets at the back of the old village street, which probably mark the edges of their tofts. To the south of Edensor there are even vaster areas of medieval-type ridge and furrow, again all once part of the village's open fields. The scale of these fields stands in strong contrast with the other side of the river, reflecting the size and importance of Edensor compared with the small hamlets on less advantaged ground beyond the Derwent.

Close to the village and also along the west bank of the river, the ridge and furrow, while reflecting medieval open field layout in general terms, lies within later rectangular fields defined by hedge banks and mostly probably last ploughed in post-medieval times. This agricultural enclosure, which had started by the early-seventeenth century at latest, continued to be developed and modified into the 1750s, or in the case of fields next to the village into the 1820s. In contrast, on the upper slopes of the park, the ridge and furrow defines cultivation strips last used in the medieval period. Some are particularly interesting in that parcels of these cut or overlie earlier strips on different orientations, showing that these upper areas were only intermittently cultivated and in this sense can be viewed as once within an 'outfield'. By the early seventeenth century at latest these upper areas were 'abandoned' and lay within a large sheep walk which extended to the Calton Pasture ridgetop, taking in not only parts of former open field but what had been a large part of the commons of Edensor. However, these upper areas were enclosed into a series of rectangular hedged fields in the later-seventeenth or earlier-eighteenth centuries, before again being turned into unbounded grasslands as part of the radical landscape restructuring planned by Brown.

Remarkable survivals that escaped the intensive medieval agriculture, located at the edges of cultivation strips and in one case clipped by them, are two or more probably three prehistoric barrows. While these burial monuments were sufficiently large to survive, all other surface traces of pre-medieval inhabitation, including the settlement and farming that undoubtedly existed, were eradicated something like a 1,000 years ago.

Another aspect of the archaeology south of Edensor is the large number of earthworks of disused roads and drives, reflecting the power of the Estate to make radical changes within the park in the eighteenth and nineteenth centuries. For example, behind Edensor there is the sunken Jap Lane, which was the main way into the village from the direction of Calton before the radical changes to the village were made in the 1820s. Here there are still mature trees which started life in laid hedges that flanked the lane. Running northwards from One Arch Bridge at the southern end of the park there is a grassy causeway at the site of Brown's new public carriage road through the park of about 1760, made when the road up the Derwent valley was diverted away from the house to the other side of the river. Despite this being an important public road, it is only of single cart width, a strong reminder how much levels of traffic have changed, particularly from the twentieth century. This road was moved, in the mid-1820s, to the present more-sinuous route where today sometimes-continuous streams of cars make crossing hazardous. One part of the new 1820s route, just outside the village where a prominent terrace runs today, was moved again in the 1830s after the demolitions at Edensor were complete. There are also two wonderfully engineered carriage routes dating to the 1850s, known as the Serpentine Drives, which wind their way up the park, one to Moatless Plantation at Calton Pasture from where there are fine views, the other on the other side of river into Stand Wood and its ornamentalised lakes. These drives allowed the family and guests to travel by coach to enjoy the pleasures of the park, whereas in the eighteenth century access to the remoter parts was by horseback. Today, visitors to Chatsworth are given free rein to walk over large tracts of the park, to experience at close hand all that it has to offer.

It is hoped that a brief tour such as on the Sheffield 2007 Conference field visit, will succeeded in wetting the appetite for the hidden archaeological wonders of Chatsworth Park and illustrated the wealth of information about our past locked in the earthworks here. The park is one of the richest and best-preserved historic landscapes in Britain, its predominantly agricultural past character 'fossilised' in the 1760s and 1820s and thus 'preserved', while elsewhere such valuable features have often been damaged or removed by continuing agriculture. The issues and evidence are discussed in more detail in Barnatt (2005), Barnatt & Williamson (2005), and Barnatt & Bannister (in prep.).

References

Barnatt, J. (2005) Chatsworth: The transformation of a great estate landscape. In: Rotherham, I.D. (Ed) Crisis and Continuum in the Shaping of Landscape. *Landscape Archaeology and Ecology*, **5**, 5-10

Barnatt, J &Williamson, T. (2005) *Chatsworth: A Landscape History*. Windgather Press, Macclesfield

Barnatt, J. & Bannister, N. (in prep.) *The Archaeology of a Great Estate: The Chatsworth Landscape*. Windgather Press, Macclesfield

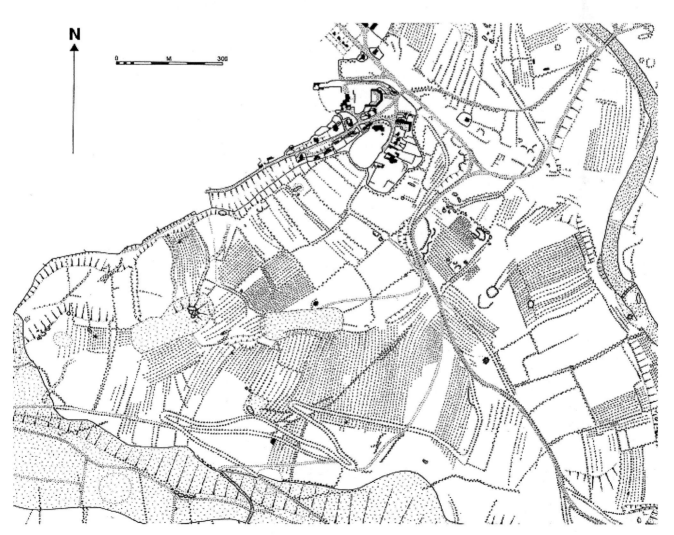

Figure 1: An example of the detailed archaeological mapping, in the Park south of Edensor, showing the richness of the pre-park archaeology.

Conservation of arachnids in ancient trees

Lawrence Bee
Environmental Studies Officer

Introduction

Unlike many invertebrates, arachnids (spiders and pseudoscorpions) are generally not particular as to the actual species of ancient tree with which they may be associated. Rather, it is the number of different structural niches available within a single ancient tree that offer arachnids a wide variety of habitat conditions.

In addition, although there are arachnids that seem to be associated only with ancient trees, this is not always the case. There are many other arachnids which appreciate the habitat niches available in trees which are perhaps less mature, but that show premature ageing characteristics e.g. holes caused by hollowing or associated decay fungi, wounds, large dead branches and loose bark.

Specific characteristics of ancient trees therefore offer particular conditions for a wide range of arachnids also recorded from other habitats, for example:

Species such as *Nuctenea umbratica* and *Amaurobius fenestralis*, often associated with deeply fissured loose bark on ancient trees are also regularly recorded from a variety of other habitats. Webs of *A. fenestralis*, particularly, may well attract the cobweb beetle *Ctesias serra*, the larvae of which feed on remains of insects left in the web by the spider.

Dead wood, lying on the ground, provides a habitat for *Segestria senoculata* to spin its tubular web in empty larval tunnels.

Old birds' nests and squirrels' dreys, areas of epicormic growth where dry litter and detritus can build up provide suitable habitats for *Harpactea hombergi* and some *Linyphiid* species notably *Lepthyphantes leprosus*.

The foliage of ancient trees provides habitat for some *Philodromid* species and orb web spinners such as *Araniella cucurbitina* and *Araneus triguttatus* (on broadleaves) and *Araneus sturmi* (on evergreens).

Hollow trunks offer suitable damp, shady conditions for species such as *Metellina merianae* and *Meta menardi*.

All the above species are recorded from other habitat types but it is the variety of specific niches present within and around ancient trees, which makes them particularly valuable habitats for arachnids.

Examples of notable arachnids

Certain rare and notable arachnid species in the UK appear from the known records to be associated specifically with ancient trees.

- The jumping spider *Salticus zebraneus* is nationally scarce (Notable A) being recorded only from mature trees in open woodland or on the margins of woodland clearings. This spider does not appear to be particular about the species of ancient tree, it is the presence of deeply fissured bark on old tree trunks which is the critical attraction for this species. Old trees of various species in parkland, on the margins of ancient woodland, in ancient hedgerows and even in a suburban garden have all yielded records for *S. zebraneus*. Apart from the recognised risk to ancient woodland and individual old trees from lack of management, there is an additional potential danger to this species where the tree is close to arable farmland. Here there is a distinct danger of spray drift from pesticide use affecting its continued existence.

- *Zygiella stroemi* is nationally scarce (Notable B) and is confined to old pine and oak trees. The spider spins its distinctive web on the bark of these trees, its retreat situated in a deep fissure or crack within the bark. Intensive forestry operations often surround such trees or necessitate their removal. Even where mature trees do remain - surrounded by developing forestry plantation - the formation of the deep fissures in the bark is less likely to occur.

- *Midia midas* is an extremely rare *Linyphiid* spider designated as Nationally vulnerable (RDB2). It appears to be confined to ancient trees in some of the larger relics of royal parks e.g. Sherwood, Windsor, Hainault and Epping Forests as well as Donington Park. Its specific microhabitats within ancient trees include squirrel dreys, bird nests, and leaf litter accumulations in hollow trunks. In Sherwood, one individual male was recorded in 1980 after extensive survey work involving the placing (and subsequent examination after some months) of around 200 artificial birds' nests in the hollow trunks and branches of some of the oldest oaks in the forest. Evidence from work in Epping Forest suggests the spider favours birds' nests and squirrel dreys, rather than leaf litter. Ancient pollards are recognised as being particularly attractive to birds and squirrels for the construction of nests and dreys. Therefore, where possible, management and 're-pollarding' should be carried out with due regard for the habitat potential of these microhabitats.

- *Meta bourneti* is a large orb-web spider with Nationally Scarce (Notable B) status. Throughout Europe, it is generally regarded as a cave dwelling species but it has been recorded from several ancient woodland sites in the UK. It is possible that the dark, damp, spacious hollow trunks of some ancient trees will provide similar habitat conditions to those of the spider's acknowledged habitat. In Sherwood Forest, the discovery of males in close proximity to some of the largest hollow oaks would

certainly suggest this possibility, particularly when there was no evidence of extensive underground or cave habitat in the area.

Meta bourneti

- *Araniella alpica*, a small orb-web spider, is Nationally Rare (RDB3) and appears to prefer old yew and beech trees. It has occasionally been recorded from scrub and chalk grassland but always in close proximity to established woodland with mature trees. The habitat provided by a number of old trees growing in close proximity to each other appears to be of greater benefit to this species rather than that of an individual tree growing in isolation. The occurrence of trees growing together in a parkland environment would seem to favour *A. alpica*.

- *Dipoena torva* is a small *Theridiid* spider with Nationally Vulnerable (RDB2) status. In Britain, the spider is restricted to the Caledonian pine forest where it spins a small web in the deep bark fissures of old Scots Pine *Pinus sylvestris* on which wood ants moving up and down the tree trunks form its principal prey. Both the spider and its prey are threatened by the increasing afforestation of the Caledonian Pine Forest where the increase in dense shade and the resulting cooler microhabitat are detrimental to both species.

- *Philodromus margaritatus* is a Nationally Scarce (Notable B) crab spider that occurs on the trunks of trees especially those covered with lichen. The spider is superbly camouflaged against lichen and may be under recorded. Many ancient trees in parklands and on the woodland edge are able to support lichen growth where light levels are sufficient. Dense shade or heavy growth of ivy on tree trunks can be detrimental to epiphytic growth - lichens are particularly light sensitive, and where appropriate some control of ivy growth may be necessary.

- The *Dyctinid* spiders *Mastigusa arietina* and *Mastigusa macrophthalma* are both found in the nests of the two ant species closely associated with ancient trees and tree stumps - *Lasius fuliginosus* and *Lasius brunneus*. The two spiders are almost indistinguishable from each other - the only noticeable difference being the size and arrangement of the eyes. Roberts (1985a), in fact, poses the possibility that *M. arietina* and *M. macrophthalma* are two forms of the same species. He suggests that the smaller eyes of *M. arietina* are the result of an existence in the subterranean environment of the nests of *L. fuliginosus* and *L. brunneus* in hollow trees - spiders with very small or even completely absent eyes are known to inhabit cave environments. On the other hand, *M. macrophthalma* (also known to inhabit the nests of the woodland ants *Lasius umbratus* and *Formica rufa*) has been collected by the author in Sherwood Forest from under loose bark and within the hollow trunks of ancient and dead trees where the slightly brighter conditions are perhaps more suited to the *M. macrophthalma* species. The two microhabitats from which this species has been recorded can both be found in ancient tree communities where management has encouraged the conservation of the wider habitat and not just the individual trees themselves.

- Pseudoscorpion species such as *Dendrochernes cyrneus* are phoretic on longhorn beetles. The dispersal and establishment of viable populations is therefore dependant upon the presence of several ancient / veteran trees growing in proximity to each other. *D. cyrneus* was recorded by C.J.C. Pool attached to the longhorn beetle *Saperda scaleris* from Sherwood Forest in 1912. The author recorded both species (separately) in the late 1970s and 1980s from the same location. *D. cyrneus* is designated as Nationally Rare (RDB3) and favours decaying timber, often where it is exposed to the sun and the consequent increase in temperature. The species has been recorded from both standing dead and partially dead trees and also from fallen branches on the ground, predominantly in open woodland such as wood pasture or parkland. This may be the result of the longhorn beetles, on which *D. cyrneus* depends for dispersal, preferring decaying trees in a more open woodland habitat.

Dendrochernes

Managing for the conservation of arachnids

The management of ancient trees and ancient tree communities for arachnids should include:

1. Maintaining as much dead wood as possible within the individual ancient tree structure. (Some authorities suggest that, where appropriate, additional dead wood habitat can be created by, for example, ring barking selected limbs).

2. Conservation of as many microhabitat niches as possible within individual ancient trees including loose and close fitting bark (and stages in between), hollow trunk/branches, epicormic growth, scar tissue from old wounds or fallen limbs and leaf litter within hollow base of tree.

3. Preservation of birds' nests and squirrel dreys within hollow trunks and remaining crown of tree.

4. Sympathetic and appropriate management of trees to maintain maximum diversity of microhabitats should pollarding or removal of limbs for health and safety purposes be necessary.

5. Retention of fallen branches and leaf litter around the tree and allowing this and any removed timber (see 4. above) to decay *in situ.*

6. Retention of moderate ivy growth on tree trunks as cover for a range of bark dwelling invertebrates (but see above under *Philodromus margaritatus* above).

7. Establishment of a zone that is free from ploughing or intensive grazing around individual ancient trees to at least the extent of the crown.

8. Where ancient trees are sheltered within mature conifer plantations - judicious felling of mature conifers so that ancient trees do not become exposed to extremes of temperature and humidity.

9. In parkland and wood pasture landscapes, maintain the natural community of old trees and encourage as varied an age structure of trees as possible through:

- Retention of standing and fallen dead timber

- Re-pollarding lapsed pollards

- Encouragement of natural regeneration

- Allowing poor or damaged trees to remain and to decay naturally

Conclusions

One of the most significant points regarding the conservation of arachnids (and other invertebrates) in ancient trees is that a group of ancient trees growing together, as in a parkland or wood pasture setting, provide a more valuable habitat than the same number of ancient trees growing in isolation from each other. Where possible the ancient tree community, and not just individual ancient trees, should be conserved as a priority for dead wood (saproxylic) invertebrates. Wood pasture and parkland can offer the most varied

microhabitat requirements, particularly where they also include additional features e.g. some scrub layer, standing and fallen dead wood, established hedgerows (as shelter belts), flowering trees and shrubs (as nectar sources for a variety of invertebrates forming potential arachnid prey) and some natural regeneration. The conditions that are most conducive for invertebrates of both established woodland and open grassland are present in a well-managed wood pasture or parkland setting. These habitats should be a priority for invertebrate (and arachnid) conservation.

References

Bratton, J.H. (Ed.) (1991) *British Red data Books 3: invertebrates other than insects.* Joint Nature Conservation Committee, Peterborough

Colenutt, S. (2003) *Managing Priority Habitats for Invertebrates Vol. 2 Arachnida - Spiders and Pseudoscorpions.* Buglife / Defra, Bristol

Jones, P.E. (1978) *Report on Pseudoscorpions - British Arachnological Society Arachnid Survey of Sherwood Forest September 1978* (Unpublished report)

Kirby, P. (1992) *Habitat management for Invertebrates: a practical handbook.* Royal Society for the Protection of Birds, Sandy

Merrett, P. (1990) *A Review of the Nationally Notable Spiders of Great Britain.* Joint Nature Conservation Committee, Peterborough

Read, H. (2000) *Veteran Trees: A Guide to Good Management.* English Nature, Peterborough

Roberts, M.J. (1985a) *The Spiders of Great Britain and Ireland. Volume 1.* Harley Books, Colchester

Roberts, M.J. (1985b) *The spiders of Great Britain and Ireland. Volume 3.* Harley Books, Colchester

Roberts, M.J. (1987) *The spiders of Great Britain and Ireland. Volume 2* Harley Books, Colchester

Roberts, M.J. (1995) *Spiders of Britain & northern Europe.* Harper Collins, London

Securing a future for our parkland ancient and veteran trees

Jill Butler
Conservation Policy Officer, Woodland Trust

Introduction: A brief history of heritage trees in the UK

The UK retains many thousands of ancient and veteran trees as well as trees that are important culturally. We also recognise champions i.e. girth size and height, for different species as heritage trees. Some are individuals of great antiquity such as the Fortingall Yew, which some experts believe, is 5000 years old. If so, it is intriguing that this tree grows in the middle of Scotland - how or why is it there? There are 1,300 yews recorded on the Ancient Yew Group's gazetteer **www.ancient-yew.org** website linked to 1,000 different locations. Many are associated with churchyards or old burial sites.

A legacy of William the Conqueror (from 1066) and his *Forest Law* (legislation that is nearly 1,000 years old and yet is still significant in the heritage importance of the UK landscape today), the UK has some wonderful places with thousands of ancient trees. These include Windsor Great Park, Savernake Forest, Sherwood Forest (home to the legendary Robin Hood) and of course the New Forest. However, there is no recognition of these historic landscapes in either heritage or biodiversity designations. The trees within these areas are only 'protected' through the goodwill of the owners.

The great English Landscape designers such as William Kent, 'Capability' Brown and Humphry Repton recognised the importance of the ancient and veteran trees in giving their new landscapes depth and character.

"*The man of science and of taste will... discover the beauties in a tree which the others would condemn for its decay; he will rejoice when he finds two trees whose stems have grown so near each other that their branches have become interwoven... Sometimes he will discover an aged thorn or maple at the foot of a venerable oak; these he will respect, not only for their antiquity; being perhaps coeval with the father of the forest, but knowing that the importance of the oak is comparatively increased by the neighbouring situation of these subordinate subjects...*" Humphry Repton '*Observations on the Theory and Practice of Landscape Gardening*' (1803).

Old and ancient trees were such a status symbol that great artists such as Thomas Gainsborough were painting portraits of wealthy owners with their trees as a regular occurrence.

In parallel with the ancient and veteran trees of the wealthy, pollard trees were common in the landscape as working trees for everyday use. Such trees lost much of their value when coal arrived but in being abandoned, some have survived until today as wonderful trees.

The first records of 'tree hunting' dates from John Evelyn's Silva written in 1664, but the first prolific tree measurer in the UK was John Claudius Loudon. He recorded 500 historical trees in his eight-volume *Arboretum et Fruticetum Britanicum* (1834-37). By the early 1900s, Elwes and Henry had more than 3,500 records in the *Trees of Britain and Ireland*. Now the Tree Register of Britain and Ireland, **www.tree-register.org** has a unique register comprising details of more than 150,000 trees.

Securing a future for heritage trees in the UK

Having survived for hundreds if not thousands of years and given us great value, these trees are now seriously threatened. Nor is there a significant trend to provide an ancient tree heritage for future generations to enjoy. There may be planting or regeneration of trees to create new plantation woods but only very limited recognition of the importance of open grown 'parkland' trees. There is little understanding of the importance of how to generate light demanding tree-rich woods or the 'ancient' type of Forest of William the Conqueror.

The Government Agency which advised on conservation of the natural heritage in England, English Nature, led a *Veteran Trees Initiative* from 1996-2000 to raise awareness of the importance of these trees. This was a partnership of six organisations including the Ancient Tree Forum, a charity, the National Trust, and four English Government Agencies. When the *Veteran Trees Initiative* ended, the Ancient Tree Forum turned to the Woodland Trust to be a key partner in taking forwards a new initiative: *Securing the Future of Ancient Trees*. This is a three-pronged approach:

- Gaining recognition of the importance of ancient and veteran trees in their own right and for our heritage, landscape and biodiversity

- Engaging with people to help us map all the ancient trees across the UK

- Encouraging owners and managers to give ancient trees the very best care and attention

Achievements so far

There have been some significant changes in policy and guidance with *Planning Policy Statement 9: Biodiversity and Geological Conservation*. This strengthened protection for aged and veteran trees in England: '*Aged or veteran trees found outside ancient woodland are also particularly valuable for biodiversity and their loss should be avoided. Planning authorities should encourage the conservation of such trees as part of development proposals*.' A copy of the leaflet '*Conserving the past - ensuring the future - a planner's guide to ancient woods and trees in England*' is available as a pdf from **http://www.woodland-trust.org.uk/publications/index.htm**

The *British Standard 5837 Trees in relation to construction* has also helped. The revised recommendations allow trees to be assessed for their quality and value in regard to their cultural and conservation importance ie historical, commemorative or other value (veteran trees or wood pasture). Furthermore, a greater root protection area for such trees is now possible based on twelve times the diameter of the tree at breast height up to a maximum of 15m. Unfortunately, this may still be too little. The Ancient Tree Forum and the Woodland Trust do not believe that this is sufficient safeguard.

British Standard 3998 Tree Work is still under review but will prove to be important.

The *UK Woodland Assurance Scheme (FSC)* increased protection for veteran and ancient trees and deadwood.

English Nature Research Report 628: Development of a veteran trees site assessment protocol was an important document from the former agency. This protocol recognises the importance of sites primarily based on the numbers of veteran and ancient trees and trees with a dbh (diameter at breast height) greater than 1.5m.

Changes in legislation are being sought in each country: England, Scotland, Wales, and NI. These are to:

- Create National Registers of Trees of Special Interest

- Amend Tree Preservation Order legislation, e.g. in England and Wales remove current exemptions for trees that are dead, dying, or dangerous

- Widen the scope of the Registers of Historic Parks and Gardens to recognise historic Forests and traditional orchards

- Provide greater protection for trees in Historic Parks and Gardens

Mapping a future for ancient trees

The Ancient Tree Hunt (ATH - **www.ancient-tree-hunt.org.uk**) involves thousands of people in finding and mapping all the fat, old trees across the UK. It will create a comprehensive living database of ancient trees and it is the first step towards cherishing and caring for them. The ATH began in 2004, as a joint venture with the Tree Register of the British Isles and the Ancient Tree Forum, and has already collected more than 6,000 records. Now, thanks to additional funding from The Heritage Lottery Fund and the Esmee Fairbairn Foundation, it is stepping up a gear. With help from networks of many partner organisations and individuals, the aim is to record at least 100,000 ancient trees throughout the UK by 2011. This is a £1.3 million project and we have so far raised more than £900K.

This is a partnership project building on all the initiatives currently underway across the UK. The intention is to develop the UK database so we can assess how best we can secure the future of these trees. The information gathered will help to identify the most valuable trees to protect, monitor the rate of loss of important trees, and support the lobbying for changes. The latter include incentives and grants to help owners look after ancient trees.

- Improving the management of our ancient trees through financial incentives and advice

- New agri-environment schemes in parts of the UK allow funding for management of individual heritage trees or habitats such as wood pasture and parkland

- Funds from Landfill Tax have been used to release ancient trees from competition from plantations

- Events and workshops for owners and advisors to make them aware of positive management for heritage trees

- Information via websites **www.ancient-tree-forum.org.uk** or through leaflets and publications, e.g. Ancient Tree Guides. Catch up with the video blog - Ted and Jill's Tree-mendous Adventures

We can compare this with Sweden where there is now a ten-year *Action Plan for Trees with Special Values*. The Swedish Government has set aside £35m to this project to map all the veteran and ancient trees in the country and to provide funding for management.

The Woodland Trust and the Ancient Tree Forum

The Woodland Trust is the UK's leading charity dedicated solely to the protection of our native woodland heritage. By acquiring woodland sites, we bring them into our care and protection. Many of our woods were previously under threat from development pressure or unsympathetic management. Woodland Trust woods are managed in sympathy with wildlife and public enjoyment. Our Woodland Officers organise their specialist care throughout the UK.

We also replace those woods that have been lost to landscape and create more new native woodland than practically anyone else in the UK. The Woodland Trust uses its experience and authority in conservation to influence others who are in a position to improve the future of native woodland. This includes government, other landowners, and like-minded organisations. In 1993, a group of enthusiasts, both professional and amateur, who recognised how special elderly trees were, came together to form the Ancient Tree Forum, a registered charity. They wanted to act as champions for the ancient tree cause, campaign for their protection, promote best conservation practice and spread the word about their importance.

Our heritage trees in the UK and across continental Europe are incredibly important biologically, aesthetically, for looking back and understanding the past and for a sustainable future for wildlife. They engage people in so many ways. The message behind this paper is *'let us work together to help secure their future'*.

Deer Parks in Scotland - a neglected heritage

Christopher Dingwall
Guidelines

Introduction

In contrast to Dr John Fletcher, with whom I have been privileged to work on the subject of deer parks in Scotland in the last few years, I confess that I know comparatively little about the subject of deer parks and their management. Nor am I a medievalist. My perspective on parks is that of the garden historian, with an interest in deer parks as an element of the designed landscapes that developed alongside high status houses in Scotland. This takes in both royal palaces and houses of the nobility and gentry from the late medieval period onwards. I should also explain that what I have to say is not the result of a particular or focused piece of research, but rather a series of observations and reflections. These are prompted by the fact that in my fifteen years working as a garden historian north of the Border, I have often happened across deer parks in the course of my research.

First, I must make it clear that I am referring to deer 'parks' as fenced or walled enclosures, as distinct from deer 'forests' or 'reserves', which were the primary focus of John Gilbert's study *Hunting and Hunting Reserves in Medieval Scotland* (1979), the only substantial piece of scholarship on the subject, published nearly thirty years ago. Gilbert's excellent and detailed study does touch lightly on the subject of parks, but focuses mainly on royal parks such as those to be found at Stirling and Falkland, and says very little about the wider picture, or about events and developments after about 1500.

The Deer Parks of Scotland

In studying the subject north of the Border, it is necessary to be aware of differences in terminology to be found in the historical record, particularly in the use of the term 'park'. In a country where much of the countryside remained unenclosed until well into the eighteenth century, the term 'park' was used fairly indiscriminately in Scotland, from quite an early date, to describe any enclosure associated with a house, often with a qualifying prefix to denote its particular purpose, character or association. Thus references can be found to sheep parks, cow parks, hay parks, broom parks and the like, as well as to deer parks, clearly intended to define their function. They also refer to stony parks, meadow parks and the like, descriptive of the ground conditions; or even to such things as washhouse parks, dovecote parks and the like, indicating their position within an estate. The term 'park' was even used to describe plantations of trees, giving us names such as fir park, oak park, and willow park. By the seventeenth century the term 'park' was sometimes used in association with the Scottish term 'policies', a word dating back at least as far as the sixteenth century, derived from the Latin word *politus* meaning 'embellished', and which describes the wider ornamental planting around a house. The two words 'park' and 'policies' used in combination are therefore equivalent, perhaps, to the Irish term '*demesne*'. Thus it was that around 1620 that the Marquis of Huntly is said to have "...*given himself wholly to policie, planting and building [and to have] parked about*" his seat of Gordon Castle, in Morayshire. Another deer park of similar date with turf-topped walls 6½ feet high was recorded at Finlarig on Lochtayside, seat of the Earls of Breadalbane, nearly two centuries on as still being "...*a sufficient and strong fence*".

It has been suggested, indeed, I heard none other than Dr Oliver Rackham, suggest at a recent talk which he gave at Melrose in the Scottish Borders, that deer parks were something of a rarity in Scotland. It was suggested that the emphasis north of the Border was on the hunting of deer in more extensive 'forests' such as Ettrick Forest and Jedforest in the Borders, or in Atholl, Mar and Mamlorne in the Grampians. Gilbert (1979) cites plenty of evidence for the evolution and management of these so-called forests or reserves from the twelfth century through to around 1500. It is not difficult to identify residual evidence of their existence, for example in long-established place-names such as Huntford, Hindhope and Brownhartlaw at the head of the Kale Water, or Buccleuch, Hartwoodmyres and Greyhound Law by the Ettrick Water, to be found in the Scottish Borders. These are names that appear on Johan Blaeu's maps of the mid-seventeenth century, to which I refer later.

However, I cannot help feeling that this supposed paucity of deer parks north of the Border has as much to do with the lack of research into the subject as within anything else. We know of the existence and management of the royal hunting parks from the entries in Exchequer Rolls and Treasurers' Accounts for Scotland, and from other sources cited by Gilbert. We know from written sources that Robert the Bruce, in his enforced retirement in the early seventeenth century, is said to have spent time at Cardross near Dunbarton. Here he was indulging himself in the kingly pursuits of hunting and hawking, and in "...*enlarging the castle, repairing the park walls and ornamenting the garden*", implying, perhaps, a close contiguity between these three landscape elements. What is probably the earliest image of a deer park in Scotland is found in the view of the Abbey and Palace of Holyrood made by an English spy in 1544, in the background of which is seen the recently built wall surrounding the hunting park surrounding Arthur's Seat - another juxtaposition of house, gardens and park. This same combination is seen yet again in a later view of Falkland Palace made by Alexander Kierincx in about 1630, in which the impaled and well-wooded royal hunting park of Falkland is clearly depicted, shortly before the great oak trees were felled by Cromwell's troops to build a fortification in nearby Perth.

Evidence

Some of the best cartographic evidence for the existence of these and other parks is that to be found in the early manuscript maps of Timothy Pont, most of which date from the 1590s, and which formed the basis of the maps later published by Johan Blaeu in his *Atlas Novus* of 1654. Prominent on Pont's map of Lanarkshire is the Cluniac Abbey of Paisley where we know from other records that, as early as 1498 Abbot George Shaw built a mile long wall of dressed stone "...*enclosing the church, the precincts of the convent, the gardens and a little park for deer*". Another park with strong ecclesiastical connections was that of Laighwood which, along with the nearby sixteenth century Castle of Clunie, was for a time a seat of the Bishop of Dunkeld in Perthshire. Nor, it seems, were the Scots nobility and gentry to be outdone in the business of forming parks. Several are depicted on Pont's map of Scotland's Central Valley - for example at Callendar House, by Falkirk where the outline of the park depicted on Pont's map has remained virtually unaltered for at least 400 years, and can still be traced on the ground today. Not far away is Cumbernauld Castle, though almost all traces of its park, so clearly defined by Pont, have now disappeared. Sadly, too, many of Pont's manuscripts have been lost, giving us only partial coverage of the country.

The first national coverage is to be found in Johan Blaeu's *Atlas Novus*, first published in 1654, though the maps in this were largely based on Pont's manuscripts of some fifty years earlier. They probably give a fair impression of the state of country towards the end of the sixteenth century. Although we cannot be confident without the benefit of further evidence, that every impaled park or wood depicted by Blaeu was made for the purpose of containing deer, a good many of them surely were. Blaeu's map of the Lothians shows some forty-five impaled parks of varying size within a short distance of Edinburgh. A similar scatter of impaled parks is seen, for example, in Blaeu's depiction of lowland Ayrshire and of the Solway Coast in Dumfries and Galloway, still others in the Scottish Borders.

Cartographic evidence can be backed up with early descriptions such as those to be found in *Macfarlane's Geographical Collections* (1906), mostly from the late seventeenth century and early eighteenth century. At Fetteresso in the south of Aberdeenshire for example, were found not only "...*gardens and orchards extremely well-fenced by nature*", but also "... *a noble deer park having the Water of Carron running through the middle of it ... altogether three miles in circumference being enclosed with a very good stone wall and well stocked with a peculiar sort of fine deer brought from the Isle of Arran*". Gordon Castle in Morayshire was said to possess "...*charming gardens and an extensive park enclosed with a strong wall, in four divisions, for the rearing of deer, of which two kinds are here in abundance*". In the south-west was Morton Castle, close to the modern estate. Castle of Drumlanrig was a fourteenth century park "...*built by Sir Thomas Randulph on the face of a very great and high hill so artificially, that by the advantage of the hill all wild beasts such as Deer, Harts Roes, and Hares did easily leap in but could not get out again*".

English agent John Macky, who toured Scotland in the 1720s, noted the aforementioned park of Holyrood in Edinburgh "...*about four miles in circumference, walled around with a stone wall, but what is very comical, there is neither deer nor tree in it*". At Leslie, Macky observed the house standing "...*in the middle of the park, surrounded with a stone wall, of six miles circumference ... extremely well planted with full-grown trees, that at a distance, seem to be a large wood*". While at Falkland, he lamented the loss of the park, formerly eight miles in circumference, and its oak trees where he spoke of seeing "...*the park ploughed up, and only here and there some of the pales left*".

The best-known surviving examples of wooded parks belonging to the nobility and gentry are probably those found in Lanarkshire and Lothians. The first in the Hamilton High Parks, where some of the ancient parkland trees, known today as the Cadzow Oaks, are believed to date from as early as the fifteenth century. Not far from Edinburgh in the deer park at Dalkeith Palace are veteran trees, known to date back three centuries or more. Elsewhere the evidence for parks is more archaeological in character, in the form of park boundaries, usually ditches and embankments or remnants of park walls, which can be seen at places such as Morton Park, at Laighwood near Dunkeld, and King's Park by Stirling. There are also examples of deer parks created in the seventeenth, eighteenth, and nineteenth centuries, as those at Hopetoun House in West Lothian, Castle Semple in Renfrewshire and Cumloden in Wigtownshire. As that great aesthete and arbiter of taste, the Rev. William Gilpin observed on the subject of park scenery in his *Remarks on Forest Scenery* (1791) "*Nothing gives a mansion so much dignity as these home demesnes, or contributes more to mark its consequence. A great house, in a course of years, naturally acquires a space around it. A noble park therefore is the natural appendage of an ancient mansion.*"

Recent research and scholarship, typified by the likes of Prof. Charles McKean's book *The Scottish Chateau: The Country House of Renaissance Scotland* (2001) has done much to change our understanding and perception of late medieval and Renaissance architecture in Scotland. I wonder if the same level of attention devoted to the subject of deer parks might cause us to question received wisdom in much the same way. It is surely significant that, of the fifteen or so houses described in Chapter 2 of McKean's book as "...*premier seats of the first rank nobility*", the majority are known to have possessed deer parks. Among the sources which he quotes is a description of Hamilton Palace, in Clydesdale, dating from 1641, by an English traveller, which spoke of "...*the parke well stor'd with all such game the clymate could afford*". Surely this is a feature intended as a reflection of the wealth, status, and good taste of its noble owner, and as something that could be imitated or aspired to by those of equal or lesser rank. As Richard Muir suggested in his book *Ancient Trees, Living Landscapes* (2005)"...*not only did the ornamental landscape display the lord's home and stronghold to maximum effect, it also served as setting for enjoying flowers and herbs, as a place for dalliance ... and for the playing of games. A key feature of the carefully manipulated setting was the deer park, where the men, and sometimes their ladies too, could vent their aristocratic lust for blood, and practise their martial skills*".

Conclusions

Finally, and in spite of what seems to be a comparative abundance of evidence, features of the parks such as those I have described, are rarely included in the county-based *Sites and Monuments Records*, or in the surveys of historic monuments carried out by the Royal Commission on the Ancient and Historical Monuments of Scotland. The result is that they go largely unrecorded and unrecognised as part of Scotland's cultural landscape. A consequence is that without the legal protection afforded to other facets of the cultural heritage, they are peculiarly vulnerable to damage e.g. through the robbing of stone for the construction and/or repair of dykes and roads, through the felling of old woodland, or through ploughing as a result of conversion of land from pasture to arable cultivation. In this connection, I cite Holydean, not far from Jedburgh in the Scottish Borders as an example. Here was a park created on the former monastic lands of Kelso Abbey by the Kerr family, most probably around the sixteenth century, as part of the process of self-aggrandisement which led to their eventual ennoblement as Dukes of Roxburghe. As late as the 1850s, the *Ordnance Survey Name Book* for the Parish of Bowden described sections of "...*a stone dyke or wall, built without lime or cement of any kind, which encloses about 500 acres of the farm of Holydean, and has stood upwards of 300 years, and is still a tolerably good fence. It has, at first, been six or seven feet high with cope stones*". Although substantial traces of this park and its wall were to be found within living memory, the sale of the park, the felling of Holydean Wood and the conversion of the land to intensive arable within the last twenty-five years or so has resulted in the destruction of much of the physical evidence of its former extent. Without the recognition that they deserve, and more effective protection, I fear that other parks that may share the fate of Holydean.

I must apologise if what I have written seems rather inconclusive, and short on detail. This is in part due to the fact that my own research into the subject of deer parks is still at an early stage. My pursuit of them has been more of a relaxing recreation and an excuse for 'stout tramps' with John Fletcher along sections of surviving park pales in different parts of the country, in contrast to other more pressing contract work. However, as the title of my paper suggests, I feel very strongly that deer parks are a sadly neglected aspect of Scotland's cultural landscape, and one that is in real need of focused and systematic research to build on the foundations laid by Gilbert nearly thirty years ago.

Select Bibliography

Blaeu, J. (1654) *Atlas Novus*. Amsterdam (recently reprinted as *The Blaeu Atlas of Scotland*. (2006) Birlinn, Edinburgh

Gilbert, J.M. (1979) *Hunting and Hunting Reserves in Medieval Scotland*. John Donald, Edinburgh

Gilpin, Rev. W. (1834) *Remarks on Forest Scenery and other Woodland Views*. Edited by Sir. T.D. Lauder, Edinburgh

Macky, J. (1723) *A Journey through Scotland*. London

McKean, C. (2001) *The Scottish Chateau: The Country House of Renaissance Scotland*. Sutton Publishing, Stroud

Mitchell Sir, A. (Ed.) (1906) *Geographical Collections Relating to Scotland made by Walter Macfarlane*. Scottish History Society, Edinburgh

Muir, R. (2005) *Ancient Trees, Living Landscapes*. Tempus, Stroud

Natural England - crusader for the environment (Poster)

Joy Ede
Natural England

Abstract

Natural England has four strategic outcomes:

- A healthy natural environment

- Sustainable use of the natural environment

- A secure environmental future

- Enjoyment of the natural environment

Natural England has been formed by bringing together English Nature, the landscape, access, and recreation elements of the Countryside Agency and the environmental land management functions of the Rural Development Service. Our objective is to conserve and enhance England's natural environment - including the landscape, biodiversity, geology and soils, natural resources, cultural heritage and other features of the built and natural environment. We also have the responsibility to help people enjoy, understand, and access the environment.

Protection and enhancement of the landscape and its historic environment is at the core of Natural England's purpose. Medieval parklands clearly therefore sit happily within Natural England's remit.

The chief mechanism for Natural England to help protect and enhance medieval parklands is through agri-environmental schemes - previously Environmentally Sensitive Area and Countryside Stewardship Schemes, now through Environmental Stewardship. Environmental Stewardship is an agri-environment scheme that provides funding to farmers and other land managers in England who deliver effective environmental management on their land.

It has two parts:

- **Entry Level Scheme** is a 'whole farm' scheme open to all farmers and land managers. Acceptance will be guaranteed provided scheme requirements are met.

- **Higher Level Scheme** that aims to deliver significant environmental benefits in high priority situations and areas. It is therefore highly competitive.

Examples of medieval parks where agri-environment grant aid has helped ensure the protection of these valuable landscapes and their associated biodiversity are Moccas park, Herefordshire; Killerton, Devon; Bradgate, Leicestershire and Borringdon, Devon.

Management actions which can be grant aided include appropriate grazing - for instance to reduce poaching and compaction around veteran trees and to maintain or improve grassland diversity; tree surgery; boundary restoration; earthwork repairs; scrub management; interpretation and access.

Borringdon. Stone-faced medieval park pale requiring scrub management, and restoration in places (© Bryn Thomas, Natural England)

Salcey. Veteran tree condition enhanced by arable reversion (© Julian Key, Natural England)

Salcey Lawn, an original open area within the medieval Salcey Forest, has a Countryside Stewardship Scheme agreement which is helping to restore the medieval aspects of the Lawn by grant aiding reversion from arable of the Lawn area and providing fencing and water - necessary for grazing this reverted area.

The medieval bank and ditch surrounding Borringdon Park, once a medieval deer park, has become overgrown with scrub and in places requires restoration of the bank and its stone-facing (which is possibly a later development). Grant aid through Higher Level Stewardship is helping to enhance the condition of this fantastic earthwork to ensure its survival into the future.

Natural England also works with land owners to ensure appropriate management of medieval parks that are Sites of Special Scientific Interest. It also directly manages at least one medieval park - that at Moccas in Herefordshire which is a National Nature Reserve.

The rise of British deer parks: their raison d'être in a global and historical perspective

John Fletcher
Reediehill Deer Farm, Auchtermuchty, Fife

Introduction

This paper investigates the origins of medieval deer parks in Britain, and asks whether Britain was unique in possessing deer parks, why they were so numerous, what they were for and how they were used. In order to answer these questions I have tried to place them within an international context and a historical continuum. Finally, I have briefly attempted to compare the Scottish with the English deer parks.

How many parks were there in medieval Britain?

Estimates that between 1,000 and 3,200 English medieval deer parks existed when the human population was only around four million indicate an astonishing figure of one deer park for every one to two thousand people (Bazeley, 1921; Cantor, 1982; Thirsk, 1997; Rackham, 2001). This massive commitment of resources to the construction of parks must reflect medieval priorities.

So why were they built?

Some historians have likened deer parks to the modern deer farm thus implying a utilitarian purpose, (Birrell, 1992; Rackham, 2001) but medieval parks cannot easily be justified solely by the nutritional value of the venison produced.

We can estimate the amount of venison a medieval deer park might have been able to produce. Putman and Langbein (Putman, 2003) found that existing English and Welsh deer parks had a winter stocking density of up to eight fallow deer per hectare. We can estimate the amount of venison a medieval deer park might have been able to produce. Putman and Langbein (Putman, 2003) found that existing English and Welsh deer parks had a winter

stocking density of up to eight fallow deer per hectare. We can take a figure of three adult fallow does per hectare (1.5 per acre) for a park in which venison production is a priority. Assuming all deer are killed as yearlings and the number of males retained for breeding is only one per twenty females, then with a fawning percentage of 80%, and accounting for replacement breeding females and 3% mortality, it might be possible to take annually about 200 yearlings from 100 hectares. This theoretical value is almost one yearling per acre. My guess is that if the park were to be hunted in a relatively unselective way with no control of unproductive females and with more males than would be actually required to cover the does then a park would be doing well to achieve even half of that figure. Thus, a park in which the deer had access to 200 acres of reasonable quality grazing might yield around 80 venison carcasses per annum of a weight of 40-50 kilograms which when eviscerated, skinned and jointed might yield 20 kilograms of meat thus providing 1.6 tonnes of meat per 200 acres. If we imagine a household of fifty consuming half a kilogram of meat per head per day the venison from a 200-acre park, this would only last two months. But if the venison was restricted to the high table and reserved for celebrations as Dyer (1983) has suggested from his studies of medieval household accounts it could last the year round. Birrell (2006) provides valuable indications of the annual consumption of various classes of household from around 200 for the Earls of Lancaster to fifty for a Bishop in the late thirteenth and early fourteenth centuries. The numbers would be halved if the deer were red though the yield would be similar.

My figures are highly simplified. The herd structure would dramatically alter the venison off-take since males are unproductive but are likely to be retained in higher numbers than is justified for breeding since the prestige of hunting clearly rated males higher than females. The age at which the deer were killed, the level of winter-feeding, the quality of the grazing, the extent of woodland, the loss of grazing to cattle, sheep, *etc*, would all have a significant impact on the productivity of a park.

Jean Birrell (2006) has recently tried to quantify the numbers of deer in parks and estimated their yield. The various records she cites indicate around 500 deer per 1,000 acres of parkland that may be broadly in accord with my calculations. We must remember however that a count may or may not include fawns depending on the time of year. Counts may have been made after the hunting season or before it; some counts may have simply recorded adult females. Do the estimates refer to red or fallow? Each one of these factors could independently make a difference of up to 100%.

Like the venison, the ability to yield timber in the parks must have been hugely valued. Rackham (2001) cites a case where, in 1274, timber oaks from one English park were valued at six times that of trees from the neighbouring forest. In the mediterranean, as wild woodlands became depleted, the parks became preserves in which timber could be husbanded so that for Roman authors like Strabo and Procopius a '*paradeisos*' became a synonym for a timber reserve (Allsen, 2006). Nevertheless, it seems impossible that timber could justify the establishment of a deer park in medieval England.

If we cautiously discard the prosaic material production of meat, wood and timber as the chief *raison d'etre* then we must look elsewhere. There now seems to be a broad consensus amongst historians that the parks were medieval embellishments to the noble estate existing to enhance prestige by providing ready access to hunting and the provision of a meat of the very highest status as a gift commodity. Like the North American potlatch feasts, conspicuous display of expenditure-enhanced prestige in proportion to the size of

the investment and even, it has been suggested, in inverse proportion to its utility. Clearly if this analysis is correct, the pursuit of hunting, and especially the quarry and even the meat must have had cultural significance to a degree that it is very difficult for us now to comprehend.

Accessible works by Cummins (1988) and Almond (2003) have helped the modern reader to grasp the practice and the ritual of medieval European hunting whilst others (Thiebaux, 1974; Bath, 1992; Makkay, 2006) have described the iconic status of the quarry, deer, and the hunt and their role in myth, and religious and literary symbolism, in courtly love and in iconography. The philosophical importance of hunting has been much discussed, for example: Scruton (1998), Ortega y Gasset (1942). As a veterinarian working with deer I would like to speculate from a biological perspective why hunting has such a very deep-seated place in the human psyche.

In the early part of the last century, Darwinism and its implications finally achieved widespread acceptance, and with this came the proposal that hunting by humans might have an 'instinctive' basis. Notions of the 'killer ape' and 'man the hunter' were aired by Washburn and Lancaster (1968) but soon rebutted because of the central role they gave to man and the subsidiary role of the female (Tanner and Zihlmann, 1976). Subsequent analysis has corrected that simplistic approach and the role of hunting in human evolution has been rehabilitated (Stanford, 1999). The concept still arouses passion. As late as 1993, Cartmill, in a swingeing critique of hunting, dismissed any evolutionary explanation as '*primitivist fantasy*' but the only argument that he could bring to bear was the obscure ground that historically hunting has been formalised and surrounded with ritual but that it is now an '*informal business*' (Cartmill,1993). Even so the hunting of deer within North America remains colossal: '*one of every three Wisconsin males over the age of 12 hunts deer*' (Nelson, 1997).

With the growing realisation that chimpanzees, our closest non-human relatives, sharing more than 98% of our genetic material, are not the peace loving vegetarians we once thought but regularly hunt *Colobus* monkeys, the debate has been re-opened (Stanford, 1999). Hunting monkeys consumes more calories than it provides but the flesh of the quarry is so much esteemed, every last morsel being rapidly consumed, that the successful hunter can use it to gain access to oestrous females and socially manipulate its peers using what have been described as Machiavellian strategies (Stanford, 1999). Therefore, it has been suggested quite plausibly, that hunting may have had a key role in the development of social structure and hierarchy in primates and even in early hominids.

The weight of current scientific thinking also seems to favour the theory that the ingestion of animal protein, whether derived from scavenging or from hunting, was essential for the evolution of human cranial capacity. In any case, it is clear that hunting played a crucial part in sustaining our ancestors from the appearance of the first hominids perhaps two million years ago until the advent of domestication and after. '*Over much of the continent human groups exploited deer populations consecutively for 5000 years or more. Indeed over large areas of southern Europe, the relationship lasted more in the region of 50,000 years.*' (Jarman, 1972).

Early human hunting strategies

We know little of how hunting was organised in prehistory although there is an abundance of arrowheads, lance tips, throwing spears etc to indicate the ways animals were killed. To be effective hunting people must attempt to think themselves into the persona of their prey. Our knowledge of modern hunting societies demonstrates the importance of hunting in the evolution of belief systems and religion (Vitebsky, 2005). If royalty was later to espouse successful hunting as a means of impressing its subjects then conversely we may imagine that in less complex societies the successful hunter would, like the chimp, accumulate prestige and acquire leadership.

There is evidence that deer may have been tamed to bring them into easy bowshot, by the feeding of browse (Jarman, 1972; Simmons and Dimbleby, 1974; Tudge,1998) Such a process would conform to the second of the three stages: predation - protection - domestication, proposed by Harris (1996) as typifying the evolution of human-animal relationships. We know that in the seventeenth century, browse was regularly fed to deer in the New Forest to bring them into enclosures and within easy range for killing (Fiennes, 1696; Fletcher, 2003). A similar strategy could have been used by Neolithic hunters to select animals for slaughter. This would also permit Neolithic societies to maintain contact with groups of deer in the late winter when they are at their most hungry and when they cast their valuable antlers. This could explain how such large numbers of antlers (as for example, were used as picks in the Neolithic flint mines at Grimes Graves), might have been collected in what was a wooded habitat. This has long been a puzzle (Clutton-Brock, 1984; Ramseyer, 2005). By feeding the deer browse on a regular basis as antler casting approached, their foraging movements could be restricted allowing much easier collection of the antlers. One further refinement would have been to contain the deer for those few weeks in a precursor to the park. In the early spring when the stags' aggression is at its nadir such an enclosure would have been eminently feasible.

It may seem over speculative to suggest that deer were managed like this in prehistory but we know that fallow deer were shipped in the early Neolithic to Mediterranean islands (Massetti, 1996, 2002, 2006).

Hunting in the historical era

The earliest accounts from a large variety of cultures indicate the importance of hunting as a means of conferring prestige on royalty. Ashurbanipal King of the Assyrians in about 2650 BP had his hunting exploits depicted on the reliefs of his palace walls (Anderson, 1985). In having game turned out for him to kill in front of his subjects, he was merely repeating history. Some of the parks of the Egyptians were used in this way, such as that depicted in the Fifth Dynasty (cc 4400 BP) wall painting at Abusir in which the monarch is firing arrows into a corral of animals collected by a ring hunt (Houlihan, 1996).

However, in most of Asia, royal hunts from the earliest accounts entailed the 'ring-hunt'. With local variants dictated by the topography and climate, the ring-hunt or drive involved a very large number of beaters, usually including the army, assisted by a corvée of retainers and a number of professional court huntsmen. The size of these forces is often assumed by historians to have been exaggerated for reasons of prestige or literary impact. However, we have enough well documented eyewitness accounts to make it clear that tens of thousands of beaters were regularly employed (Allsen, 2006). The beaters would spend many days and often weeks moving game forward slowly by day and lighting fires and sleeping in lines by night, until the animals were contained within a limited space.

Refinements such as ropes with feathers or pieces of felt attached at intervals were used to extend the distances between beaters. In later hunts that were more sophisticated the game would be finally contained within a portable park of quickly erected canvas. Occasionally these enclosures were even compartmentalised.

Figure 1: 18th century German set piece hunt

Eventually the ruler and his guests would enter the ring, usually on horseback and with bows and arrows, and start a systematic slaughter of the great variety of game that might last several days.

In the ultimate development of the ring-hunt as practised in seventeenth and eighteenth century German states, the game would be driven into a canvas enclosure containing something like a stage set. The terrified creatures would be made to emerge from a wooden building and plunge into water often from a substantial height. The king and his guests, often comfortably ensconced in a pastiche of the Bucentaur of Venice, armed with firearms, whence they could shoot the poor animals to musical accompaniment. Gluck was even commissioned to write pieces for such set piece hunts (Ergert, 1997). (Figure 1)

In medieval Western Europe, less labour intensive yet equally ritualised chases were practised as described in the hunting manual of Gaston Phoebus, Count of Foix and his successors (Cummins, 1988). Two basic forms were practised: the *par force de chiens* hunt involving the sophisticated use of hounds to pursue a single deer till it stood at bay, and the 'bow and stable' hunting in which deer were drifted slowly towards archers (Cummins, 1988; Almond, 2003). Unlike the ring-hunt where the actual killing could only be undertaken at infrequent intervals after a long preliminary, these systems of hunting allowed daily practice of martial arts for the nobility and many monarchs did indeed hunt daily for months at a time (Anderson, 1985; Cummins, 1988). As Phoebus emphasises, following the classical authors, hunting was very good for the young man in getting him out of bed in the morning and preventing his mind turning to lechery. All these hunts served to enhance royal prestige and keep the nobles fit for knightly service but the ring- hunts in Asia also had the purpose of keeping the entire army under active service and entertained together with all the baggage trains and food. They also enforced discipline since beaters allowing game to break back were often severely punished.

The Mongols with their nomadic origins in the Steppes were amongst the most avid ring-hunters and Ogodei, successor to his father, Chinggis Qan, constructed a park in Central Mongolia of clay and wood walls in the early thirteenth century. Described as being 'two days in length' the game was driven into it and hunted by the qaghan who then retired to let his nobles take their turn while he watched from a hill. His brother Chaghadai was so impressed he built a similar park in Turkestan (Allsen, 2006).

It is easy to imagine that the climax of the ring-hunt might be the precursor of the deer park, the temporary structure at the end of the drive evolving into something more permanent into which game could be driven in anticipation of the royal visit. Although that was certainly not the basis for the Persian paradises, I wish to draw on this parallel because it seems to me that some of the Scottish parks which Christopher Dingwall and I have been investigating may have been designed with this in mind. The Gaelic word *elrick* is known to have described a narrow defile or enclosure into which deer could be driven and ambushed. Some remain, including a putative one on the Isle of Rum built of stone (Love, 1987; Ansell, 2006). Deer drives by hundreds of beaters, known in Gaelic as the *tinchell*, into an elrick are common features of early Gaelic poetry and were practised into the modern period (Gilbert, 1979; Whitehead, 1980). Perhaps Scotland was unusual in Western Europe in having deer drives.Elricks or other types of enclosure into which game could be driven are found in many parts of the world. A remarkable feature remaining in the Syrian Desert, are the Neolithic 'kites' into which herds of migrating gazelle were driven for killing (Ergert, 1997).

Parks stocked with game rather than mere recipients of drives also have a long history. Neo-Babylonian texts mention several parks, the earliest being from the reign of Cyrus the Great (r.549-530) which refer to a *par-de-su* near Sippar, and Diodorus credits Semiramis, Queen of Babylon with constructing hunting parks and suggests that the practice was then taken up by the Syrians and Persians (Allsen,

2006). Famously, Xenophon in about 400 B.C.E. describes at first hand the '*palace and large park (paradeisos) full of wild animals*' in which Cyrus the Younger '*used to hunt on horseback whenever he wished to give himself and his horses exercise.*' (Anderson, 1985; Allsen, 2006). Nor were the parks the prerogative of royalty: Xenophon describes Cyrus the Great, after conquering Mesopotamia, instructing his officials to build parks and stock them with wild animals (Allsen, 2006).

Paradises were also well established in India, where Latin authors described them as grander than those in Iran. The Buddha preached his first sermon in what was reputed to have been a deer park and parks were numerous in the Mughal era (Allsen, 2006). Godfrey Mundy in his description of India in the early nineteenth century describes both Hindu and Muslim deer parks. The history of hunting parks in China is not dissimilar to that of the Middle East. The Chinese historian Mencius writing 2300 years BP recounts that King Wen the father of King Wu who founded the Zhou dynasty around 3122 BP had a hunting park seventy Chinese miles square (Schafer, 1968; Allsen, 2006).

The Persian, Chinese, and Indian parks were broadly similar: they were paradises in which gardens, water, and a great variety of wildlife were somehow integrated. Within them, the rulers were expected to perform rites such as ceremonial ploughing associated with cultivation and domestication, as well as hunting. Moreover, the parks were also repositories of plants and animals collected from the most distant regions; fruit trees and orchards abounded in the parks of both. Thus the Pere David deer (*Elaphurus davidianus*) existed in the parks of China long after its extinction in the wild and with the destruction of the Chinese parks in the nineteenth century its survival became entirely dependant on the Duke of Bedford's park at Woburn. The Roman parks described by Varro and later by Columella seem to have been designed more simply as hunting parks.

In Achaemenid Iran, the *paradeisos* became in Allsen's words '*a key institution*' and he describes how the Achaemenid concept of hunting parks was taken up by their Armenian subjects and successive dynasties from at least 200 B.C.E. until about 350 AD, each ruler constructing a new park to stamp his identity. From the Achaemenids the custom passed to the Sassanids whose parks are described by Theophanes. The Arabs subsumed the tradition of park building when they occupied Mesopotamia and Iran in the seventh century describing them in Arabic hunting manuals and chronicles (Allsen, 2006). Even as late as the Safavids (1501-1732) hunting parks were still visible in Iran and the 'Park of A Thousand Acres' in Isfahan was described by several European travellers (Allsen, 2006).

As the Arabic culture absorbed the concept of hunting parks so, when the Normans conquered Arabic Sicily, they in turn seem to have adopted deer parks. Norman Sicily and Southern Italy conquered in the 1050s were by '*the middle of the twelfth century, the richest and strongest in Western Europe*' and they seem to have retained close communications with their Norman relatives in England as Richard I '*acted as if he was master of Sicily*' (Petit-Dutaillis, 1936). In Sicily, the Normans found no red deer but wild roe and, within the parks, fallow, and they carried both the notion of hunting parks and the fallow north to Britain and Ireland.

Venison

So far, we have looked at the development of hunting and I have tentatively proposed that man has evolved a need to hunt. Now I argue, equally tentatively, that prolonged exposure to game meat has made venison a cultural icon. In addition, for the same reasons, I suggest that game with its low fat, high iron content, *etc*, is the meat to which we are physiologically best adapted.

The consummation of the hunt is the kill and the division of the spoils. As meat-eating chimpanzees value their quarry to what seems a far greater degree than its nutritional content would seem to justify, and award pieces to carefully selected recipients, so did the medieval European hunter esteem the meat of the deer. The way in which the dead deer was broken up and divided amongst the most deserving is covered by Cummins (1988) and has been elegantly related to the archaeology by Naomi Sykes (2006).

A still more formalised parallel to the behaviour of the hunting chimpanzee comes from the ancient English procedures of the royal venison warrant. This seems to originate in a charter dating from the first year of Henry I, by which the Crown annually awarded venison to various City of London officers. The royal warrant, together with fee deer traditionally awarded to park and forest officers totalled 756 by the reign of Queen Victoria, although that included sixty brace of fat bucks and a similar number of does for the Queen's table (Baxter Brown, 1985). This arcane procedure was followed annually apart from the period of the Commonwealth and the two world wars until finally abandoned by Mrs Thatcher's government in the late 1980's. Venison retained its value as a gift throughout English history. Amongst the many royal and noble donors were Henry III ,who regularly gave away 200 deer a year (Birrell, 2006), and Henry VIII. He gave venison to Anne Boleyn during their early courtship and appended a risqué letter '*Seyng my darlyng is absent I can no less do than to sende her summe flesche, representyng my name, which is harte flesche for Henry, prognosticating that hereafter, God Wyllyng, you must injoye summe of mine whyche he pleased I wolde were now...I wolde we were to gyder an evening.*' (Hackett, 1929).

In the newly formed Royal Society of the seventeenth century, honorary members were accepted on provision of a gift of venison '*not less than a haunch*' (Fletcher, 2004b). Samuel Pepys recorded eating venison seventy-six times of which eleven involve his either receiving or giving it as a gift. It was clearly deemed far superior to beef and pork since Pepys complains of '*pasty that was palpable beef which was not handsome*' on 6th Jan 1660, and '*a venison pasty which proved a pasty of salted pork*' on 17th October 1661 (Fletcher, 2004a).

It is often said that venison could not be legally sold in medieval England and there does seem to have been an unwritten code against selling venison that guided the gentry. However, in her analysis of poaching amongst medieval peasants, Birrell (1996) found very many instances of venison being sold and she suggests that many poachers may have poached with a view to sale. It seems likely the trade was significant.

In the context of parks, it has often been misunderstood how deer, together with rabbits were for many centuries legally quite distinct from game. This is why the laws controlling the meat of deer were also quite different from those concerned with game. The reasoning behind the distinction is that both deer and rabbits were normally deemed to be enclosed, a concept that we today find hard to understand when wild deer and rabbits are so numerous as to threaten many habitats. Deer were, by Forest Law, all royal property unless in a chase or a park when the landowner (who had been permitted to create those chases and parks) possessed them. Likewise rabbits which had been only introduced in the twelfth or thirteenth centuries, and had since then been kept in warrens belonged to the landowner who had the license of free warren (Munsche, 1981). From 1603 to 1827, the sale of both game and venison was made illegal and a fine of forty shillings per deer was imposed for selling venison (Munsche, 1981). The effect was merely to force sales underground and create an organised black market. It is interesting that it is still a felony to sell wild venison throughout North America.

European parks and hays

A poem ascribed to Einhard describes Charlemagne as having a park '*Not far from the peerless town are a wood and a pleasant lawn, holding in their midst a verdant glade, its meadows fresh from the streams, and encircled by many walls*' in which he went hunting '*....as he loved to do, and give chase to the wild beasts with dogs and whistling arrows, laying low multitudes of antlered stags beneath the black trees*' (Allsen, 2006). Therefore, we can see that the emperor had a walled park but the evidence for numerous baronial parks in mainland Europe seems to be missing. Within Europe, with the exception of Britain, parks were never as numerous as in the Near East. Although they were essential royal prerequisites, with the exception of Britain they did not seem to extend to nobles. In Britain, the baronial parks were, together with those belonging to the church, much more numerous than the royal parks even though Elizabeth I is said to have inherited 200 deer parks.

Such early parks as there were seem to have been associated with the word *hage* or *haia* throughout much of Western Europe. In Britain, the 'hays' appear to have been precursors to deer parks (Liddiard, 2003) but that progression from hay to park does not seem to have taken place on mainland Europe to the same extent.

Within northern Europe, much discussion has centred over the haga word in its various forms: haia, hay, haga, derhaga, *etc.* Vera (2000) and Rackham (1980) have pointed out that in order for coppices to survive browsing, animals need to be excluded and cite convex banks and hedges as fulfilling this function. It is clear that for wood pasture to survive, coppiced trees required protection for several years: they were normally cut on at least a six-year rotation. This underwood of briars, hawthorn, blackthorn, and other 'scrub' that protected the coppices was known as 'hag' - an impenetrable barrier. We can still see in many parts of central Europe woodlands containing coppice protected from deer by interlaced wooden fences. Trees protected from grazing by 'hag' or mantle and fringe vegetation as it is often known may grow to cast sufficient shade as to kill the 'hag' and produce an area of wood-pasture. Where a number of patches of 'hag' run together they may surround areas of wood-pasture to create a grove. The driving of deer into such a grove is suggested by Vera as a means of hunting.

In its original Anglo-Saxon, 'haga' or 'hege' had a great variety of meanings but common to each seems to have been the sense of an impenetrable barrier. Later, 'haye' or 'hage' is often seen in medieval English literature and much discussion has been directed at interpreting its exact meaning. 'Hedge', like the French 'haie', clearly has the same origin and the word haye also came to have the meaning of a net as might be used for trapping deer etc. It can even mean a line of people as might be used in a drive of deer.

Derhagen was used in mainland Europe to denote a hage or enclosure for deer and Hooke (1998) points out that the words 'wulfhagan' and 'swinhagan' also exist indicating that such systems of hunting, i.e. encouraging animals into the grove surrounded by a haga, were also applied to wolves and wild boar. It is but a short step from the use of a haye, i.e. the impenetrable barrier of the mantle and fringe vegetation around the edges of a grove and the making good of gaps in it by planting thorn, to the eventual excavation of a ditch to create a bank upon which the thorn could be planted. At some point, cleft oak palings supplanted the thorn.

Pre-Norman charters are cited by Rackham as mentioning hage in connexion with the capture of deer. This may have occurred, as Vera suggests, with deer chased by mounted huntsman through the surrounding haga and into the grove. It is also simple to conceive how gaps in hedges could be covered with nets into which deer could be driven. Like us, animals are creatures of habit and will, with confidence, run in the direction in which they have been accustomed to run. When I see deer hesitating as they run through an unfamiliar gate it occurs to me that they have an inbuilt reluctance to run through such a narrow space acquired through thousands of years of being killed or trapped as they do just that. Medieval pictures depicting the netting of deer and other game as they pass through gaps in hedges are common and the extension of the word 'hage' or 'haye' to include a net or cover is easy to understand.

Eventually it is suggested that the word 'haga' became effectively synonymous with the word park but simply pre-dated it. Thus, Vera points out that the Dutch city known as The Hague has a hunting lodge, the Ridderhof, as its oldest building. In the Netherlands, the city is also named s'Gravenhage meaning the 'hage' of the Duke. However, the transition of hays into fully enclosed hunting parks seems much less common on the mainland than in Britain.

It seems now to be generally accepted that, as Robert Liddiard (2003) has stated, '*There can be little doubt that Domesday Book massively under-records the numbers of parks in existence at this time.*' The general presumption now seems to be that the many hayes and haga mentioned in Domesday were actually deer parks. Whether they were all in fact fully enclosed parks or were places used for regular catching of deer we do not yet know. It is clear that deer parks proliferated in the twelfth and thirteenth centuries. An expansion that seems to parallel the introduction of the fallow deer, which, it seems most likely, came to England and Ireland from Sicily (Sykes, 2006).

If the Normans presided over this extraordinary growth in deer parks, why are there not similar developments in Normandy? Why, also, was there not a concomitant pattern of hunting parks elsewhere in Western Europe? I would like to suggest that the reason might have been in the different ways in which the Forests were defined in Norman Britain as compared to the mainland.

In mainland Europe '*forestis*' appear from the seventh century when the word is seen in Frankish and Merovingian kings' deeds of donation (Vera, 2000). The *forestis*, a word derived from the Latin '*foris*' meaning outside, was what lay outwith the clearly owned and cultivated land. First in Roman law (Codex Justinianus X) and then in Frankish law, any land not clearly owned became royal property. In a *forestis* every tree and every wild animal belonged to the king. William I is considered to have introduced the continental word 'Forest' to England for the first time but his interpretation of forests in Britain seems to have been subtly different. The Norman forests were tracts of ground with very variable degrees of woodland in which the Forest Law prevailed. Unlike on the mainland, however, the Norman Duke maintained the royal right to all wild animals even on land that did not belong to him. Thus, the crucial difference seems to be that in Britain the king owned all wild animals regardless of on whose property they were. In mainland Europe, outside the '*forestis*' the wild animals belonged to the local lord. In addition the English King sometimes declared Forests on someone else's land - thus Rackham (1986): '*The king's habit of keeping deer on other people's land was why Forests were strongly objected to by earls and barons.*' Indeed, they were a key part of the complaints against King John in *Magna Carta* and no new Forests were declared after 1215. Although, according to Rackham (1986), William established twenty-one Royal Forests, evidence for Royal hunts by Normans is rare. These Forests were to supply venison and most hunting was done by royal decree to furnish venison (Rackham, 1986).

I have been at pains to explain how powerful was the urge to hunt. It may have been that those lords who had manors on the edge of a forest felt that a park was the only option open to them if they were to be able to continue hunting and have access to venison. For within those baronial parks, in England, forest law was suspended, even if it prevailed in royal parks (Dutaillis Stubbs cited in Gilbert, 1979).

Field historians, from Oliver Rackham in 1980, Leonard Cantor in 1982 and many others, had accepted that the word haga, hage, hege, haia, *etc*, was related to the managing of deer. Rackham stated in 1986: '*The Anglo-Saxon word **derhage** is ambiguous - it normally means a hedge for keeping deer out or a device for catching them.*' Liddiard cites *Aelfric's Colluquy* written in the late tenth century in which deer are described as being driven by dogs into 'hays', which were nets. Della Hooke (1998) has also explained how some hage were several kilometre long banks which could, as she plausibly argues, have been used to direct game. They may have served as traps within

which deer could be captured and presumably usually killed. In Shropshire, Hooke tells us some hays were used specifically for capturing roe deer. This is interesting to me since roe are notoriously difficult to keep within enclosures. They are not socially equipped to form large groups because they are adapted to selectively browsing and not consuming an entirely grass based diet. As a result, they are vulnerable to parasites and can only be kept at very low density in an enclosure. Yet they can be quite easily netted. Those who have worked as biologists with wild roe have often used long nets to catch and mark roe and with good organisation, it is not difficult to catch most of the animals in a section of woodland as no doubt our hunting ancestors knew only too well.

Della Hooke has painstakingly examined pre-Norman Conquest charters and concluded that in England, at the time of Domesday, at least, a haga or haia, plural haiae, was specifically a deer enclosure. This allowed Liddiard in 2003 to state: '*the status of the haga or haia as a deer enclosure is not in any doubt*'. He has gone on to look at the listing of deer parks in the Domesday Book in detail. Noting how those parks that are listed in Domesday are all ones belonging to the highest in the land: nine, possibly eleven, of the thirty-seven belonged to the king, five to bishops or monastic houses. Interestingly, although we often imagine these early parks to have been placed away from the castle, Liddiard lists many that were close by. In addition, many are listed together with neighbouring vineyards, fishponds and mills, and may have constituted medieval ornamental landscapes (Taylor, 2000).

Scottish Parks

Both royal and baronial deer parks are recorded in Scotland from the early twelfth century and Gilbert (1979) compiled an indication of how they were managed. This was largely from the Treasurer's Accounts and the Exchequer Rolls. Gilbert also investigated the legal status of Scottish medieval parks: although baronial parks could be created without royal grant they were, according to Gilbert, not '*supposed to stock their parks by driving deer into them'.* Certainly, the deer within them, then as now, remained the property of the park's owner but once outside the park, they were *res nullius*, i.e. belonged to nobody. The role of the parker was therefore crucial. When Bannatyne, the park keeper at Falkland in 1468-9, failed to do his job his pay was withheld. The park pales were constructed in the same way as in England but in the mid fifteenth century seal of George Douglas, fourth earl of Angus, the pale is represented as of wattle. (Figure 2) According to Gilbert, fallow deer first appear in 1288x1290 when hay was bought for does in Stirling. In 1479-80, two cows were bought to provide milk for deer calves and by 1504, oats were being fed to the deer in the royal park at Falkland.

Gilbert refers to entries in the Treasurers' Accounts between 1502 and 1508 in which John Balfour used hounds to drive deer, presumably red deer, from the adjacent Lomond Hills towards the park where a 'hay yard' had been prepared for their capture by 'wynding' it. Gilbert suggests this was done by making wattle screens as in the Earl of Angus' seal. On another occasion Master Levisay, an Englishman, was responsible for catching deer by using nets to 'draw' them into what Gilbert considers was 'a temporary structure rebuilt from year to year'. Andrew Matheson was charged with building such a structure in 1504 at Falkland and also with supervising the re-

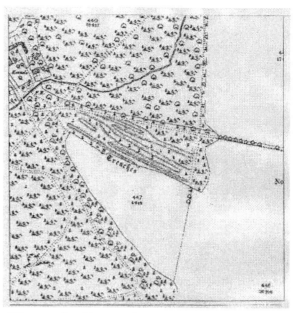

Figure 3: Chancefield trenches

building of Stirling park and this same man was responsible for transporting live deer from Falkland to restock Stirling. We cannot tell whether the deer being caught up in Falkland park were red or fallow as the park held both but the wild deer being caught in the hills were almost certainly red.

There was a regular trade in live deer that were caught in various primary locations such as the island of Little Cumbrae, the Lomond Hills above Falkland, and Torwood near Stirling, and were distributed to other parks by horse drawn litter. Since the journey from Falkland to Stirling took a minimum of three days this was no mean feat. Falkland deer park pale was eventually dismantled by Cromwell's troops as they sought to strengthen the fortifications at Perth: only one small remaining piece of the bank that once carried the pale still exists. However, a series of converging and diverging trenches between the site of the deer park and the Lomond Hills known as the Chancefield Trenches (Figure 3) has for many years puzzled antiquarians. It has now been proposed that perhaps these are the remains of a system by which deer might have been handled. Names of nearby fields, Deer Ends, and Greyhound Den have been noted by Simon Taylor (pers. comm.) and Christopher Dingwall has recently identified a very similar set of trenches adjacent to the site of Parkmill in Ayrshire. This seems to make it probable that

Figure 2: Seal of George Douglas, fourth earl of Angus

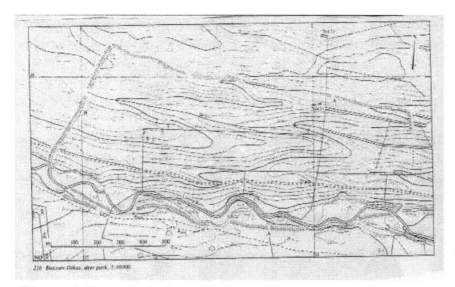

Figure 4: Buzzart Dykes

trenches were used for handling deer and it would be of great interest to know if such systems existed in relation to English deer parks or remain a Scottish idiosyncrasy.

Recent exploration of surviving Scottish deer park pales carried out with Christopher Dingwall at Morton Castle and Buzzart Dykes (Figure 4) together with the description of the Kincardine deer park by Gilbert have identified some features common to each, which may cast light on their use. All three parks are upland parks which is why their pales have not been destroyed by ploughing. As such, they may have been very different from the deer parks that formed a part of the medieval ornamental landscapes described by Taylor (2000). All three incorporate watercourses so that a significant part of each park encloses the catchment area. Although at Morton, the point at which the park pale intersects the incoming stream has been flooded by a reservoir, at the other two the pale vanishes at this point leaving a gap of one hundred metres or so.

Those familiar with wild red deer know that they have a habit of following a watercourse downhill during the evening, or if pursued, and this raises the possibility that these parks were constructed to permit the capture of deer. Scotland almost certainly carried significant populations of wild deer at a later date than in England, making such capture worthwhile. A temporary structure such as a wattle fence could easily be closed behind the deer to

prevent them breaking back. When deer farming first developed in the 1970s and 1980s in Scotland large numbers of wild breeding hinds were encouraged into fenced enclosures and then easily captured in handling systems and transported to farms.

Conclusion

With a certain amount of license, we can perhaps make a connection between the collaborative hunting expeditions of chimpanzees and the high value which they place on the resulting meat, and the esteem with which hunting is regarded by man throughout history. We can associate the techniques of hunter-gatherers with the massive drives, or ring-hunts, of the early historic period in China and Asia as well as in Scotland, and their evolution to involve more elaborate catching systems that became parks. The prestige associated with hunting is linked to the creation of hunting reserves, parks, and paradises. The paradises of the Persians were subsumed by the Arabic cultures and from Sicily, the Normans probably carried these to Britain, along with the fallow deer.

Thus, to answer the questions posed at the beginning of this tale, we can say that, yes, the parks of Britain are unique in being so numerous. This might perhaps have been associated with the Normans introducing more restrictive forest laws to Britain than those of the mainland Franks. What were the parks for and how were they used? We can say, as many others have already, that the parks were to display power. And that this may be more easily understood if we can grasp the extraordinarily all-pervasive place which hunting occupied in a great variety of cultures as exemplified by the symbolism and mythology associated with hunting, and also especially with the deer, not only in literature and the visual arts but in religion. Connected with this is the importance of venison, which was hunted not only as food, but as something also imbued with symbolism and prestige. In producing venison, the parks could guarantee that when occasion demanded this could always be put on the table of those whose goodwill was valued. When a park was exhausted, then additional deer could always be brought in through an established supply chain. Finally, although the role of British deer parks was less complex than the great Asian hunting parks, and the paradises of Persia, they had a prosaic value. They provided wood and especially timber, or grazing for horses, or many other practical uses, but crucially they still existed as an ornament and provided a private place of recreation in the full meaning of the word. In so doing, the medieval park gradually evolved into the ecological refuge and the designed landscape that we value today.

References

Allsen, T. T. (2006) *The Royal Hunt in Eurasian History*. PENN, University of Pennsylvania Press, Pennsylvania

Almond, R. (2003) *Medieval Hunting*. Sutton Publishing, Stroud, Gloucestershire

Anderson, J.K. (1985) *Hunting in the Ancient World*. University of California, Berkeley

Ansell, M. (2006) Place Name Evidence for Woodland and Hunting in Galloway and Carrick. *Scottish Woodland History Discussion Group: Notes* **XI**

Bath, Michael (1992) *The Image of the Stag - Iconographic Themes in Western Art*. Koerner, Baden-Baden

Bazeley, M. (1921) The extent of the English forest in the Thirteenth Century. *TRHS* 4th Series IV, pp. 140-172

Birrell, J. (1992) Deer and Deer Farming in Medieval England. *Agricultural History Review*, **40**, II, 112-126

Birrell, J. (1996) *Peasant deer poachers in the medieval forest*. In: Britnell, R and Hatcher, J (Eds). *Progress and Problems in Medieval England*. Cambridge University Press

Birrell, J. (2006) *Procuring, Preparing and Serving Venison in Late Medieval England*. In: Woolgar, C.M., Serjeantson, D., & Waldron, T. (Eds.) *Food in Medieval England -Diet and Nutrition*. Oxford University Press, Oxford

Cantor, L. (1982) *Forests, chases, parks and warrens*. In: Cantor, L. (Ed.) *The English Medieval Landscape*. Croom Helm, London

Cartmill, M. (1993) *A View to a Death in the Morning*. Harvard University Press, Harvard

Clutton-Brock, J. (1984) Excavations at Grimes Graves, Norfolk 1972-6. *Fascicule* **1**. British Museum Publications, London

Cummins, J. (1988) *The Hound and the Hawk - the Art of Medieval Hunting*. Weidenfeld and Nicolson, London

Dyer, C. (1983) *English diet in the late Middle Ages*. In: Aston, T. H. *et al.* (Eds.) *Social Relations and Ideas: Essays in Honour of R. H. Hilton*. Cambridge University Press, Cambridge

Ergert, B.E. (1997) *Hunting through the Ages*. In: Bluchel, K. (Ed.) *Game and Hunting*. Volume 1. Konemann, Cologne, 64-132

Fiennes, Celia (1696) *The Journeys of Celia Fiennes*. Morris, C. (Ed.) the Cresset Press, London

Fletcher, T.J. (2003) *Fletcher's Game*. Mercat, Edinburgh

Fletcher, T.J. (2004a) *The Significance of Samuel Pepys' Predilection for Venison Pasty*. In: *Wild Food* pp 122-131, Proceedings of the Oxford Symposium on Food and Cookery. Prospect Books, Totnes, England

Fletcher, J. (2006) The rise and fall of British hunting parks: some thoughts on their raison d'etre & the way they were operated with particular reference to Scotland. *Scottish Woodland History Discussion Group: Notes* **XI**

Fletcher, N. (2004b) *Charlemagne's Tablecloth.* Weidenfeld and Nicolson, London

Gilbert, J.M. (1979) *Hunting and Hunting Reserves in Medieval Scotland.* John Donald, Edinburgh

Hackett, F. (1929) *Henry VIII.* Jonathan Cape, London

Hamilakis,Y.(2003) *The sacred geography of hunting: wild animals, social power and gender in early farming societies.* In: Kotjabopoulou,E., Hamilakis,Y., Halstead,P., & Gamble,C. (Eds.) *Zooarchaeology in Greece: Recent Advances.* British School at Athens, London

Harris, D.R. (1996) *Domesticatory relationships of people, plants and animals.* In: Roy, E. & Katsuyoshi, F. (Eds.) *Redefining Nature: Ecology, Culture and Domestication.* Berg, Oxford

Hooke, D. (1998) *The Landscapes of Anglo-Saxon England.* Leicester University Press, London

Houlihan, P.F. (1996) *The Animal World of the Pharoahs.* Thames and Hudson, London

Jarman, M.R.(1972) *European deer economies and the advent of the Neolithic.* In: Higgs, E.S. (Ed.) *Papers in Economic Prehistory.* Cambridge University Press, Cambridge

Liddiard, R. (2003) The Deer Parks of Domesday Book. *Landscapes*, **1**, 4 -23

Love, J. (1987) *Rhum, the Natural History of an Island.* Edinburgh University Press, Edinburgh

Makkay, J. (2006) *The Miracle Stag in Ancient Greek mythical stories and their Indo-Iranian counterparts.* Budapest

Massetti, M.C.,Vernesi, B., Bramanti, B., & Chiarelli.(1996) RAPD fingerprinting use in the analysis of Mediterranean populations of European fallow deer, *Dama dama* Linnaeus, 1758 (Mammalia, Artiodactyla). *Hystrix* (N.S.), **8**, (1-2),113-119

Massetti, M. & Bruno, Z. (2002) The deer of the island of Lampedusa (Pelagian Archipelago, Italy): literary references and osteological evidence. *Archives of natural history*, **29**, (1), 51-66

Massetti, M., Cavallaro, A., Pecchioli, E.,& Vernesi, C. (2006) Artificial Occurrence of the Fallow Deer, *Dama dama* (L.1758),on the Island of Rhodes (Greece): Insight from mtDNA Analysis. *Human Evolution*, **21**, (2), 167-176

Munsche, P.B. (1981) *Gentlemen and Poachers - the English Game Laws 1671-1831.* Cambridge University Press, Cambridge

Nelson, R. (1997) *Heart and Blood: Living with Deer in America.* Alfred Knopf, New York

Ortega y Gasset, José (1942) *Meditations on Hunting.* Trans. Wescott, H., Scribners, New York.

Pepys, Samuel. The Diary of Samuel Pepys, a new and complete transcription ed. Robert Latham and William Matthews. (Cambridge University Press, 1971)

Petit-Dutaillis, Ch. (1908-29) Charles. Studies Supplementary to Stubbs' Constitutional History. Manchester

Petit-Dutaillis, Ch. (1936) *The Feudal Monarchy in France and England.* Kegan Paul, London

Putman, R. (2003) *The Deer Manager's Companion.* Swan-Hill Press, Shrewsbury, England

Rackham, O. (1980) *Ancient Woodland. Its history, vegetation and uses in England.* Edward Arnold, London

Rackham, O. (2001) *Trees and Woodland in the British Landscape.* Revised edtn. Phoenix Press, London

Ramseyer, D. (2005) Le cerf au Neolithique. Reflexions d'un prehistorien. *Revue de Paleobiologie, Geneve*, **10**, 185-194

Schafer,E. H. (1968) Hunting Parks and Animal Enclosures in Ancient China. *Journal of the Economic and Social History of the Orient*, **11**, 318-343

Scruton, R.(1998) *On Hunting*. Random House, London

Simmons, I.G. and Dimbleby, G.W.(1974) The possible role of ivy (*Hedera helix* L.) in the mesolithic economy of western Europe. *Journal of Archaeological Science*, **1**, 291-2966

Stanford, C. B. (1999) *The Hunting Apes - Meat Eating and the Origins of Human Behavior*. Princeton University Press, Princeton

Sykes, N.J. (2006) *The Impact of the Normans on Hunting Practices in England*. In: Woolgar, C.M., Serjeantson, D., & Waldron, T. (Eds.) *Food in Medieval England -Diet and Nutrition*. Oxford University Press, Oxford

Tanner, N.M. & Zihlmann, A.L (1976) Women in Evolution, part I: Innovation and selection in human origins. *Signs: Journal of Women, Culture, and Society*, **1**, 585-608

Taylor, C. (2000) Medieval Ornamental Landscapes. *Landscapes*, **1**, 38-55

Thiebaux, M. (1974) *The Stag of Love - the Chase in Medieval Literature*. Cornell University Press, Cornell

Thirsk, J. (1997) *Alternative Agriculture - a history from the Black Death to the Present Day*. Oxford University Press, Oxford

Tudge, C. (1998) *Neanderthals, bandits and farmers. How agriculture really began*. Weidenfeld and Nicolson, London

Vera, F. W. M. (2000) *Grazing Ecology and Forest History*. CABI Publishing, Wallingford, Oxon

Vitebsky, P. (2005) *Reindeer people - living with animals and spirits in Siberia*. Harper, London

Washburn, S.L.& Lancaster, C. (1968) *The Evolution of Hunting*. In: Lee, R.B and Devore, I . (Eds.) *Man the Hunter*, Aldine, Chicago

Whitehead, G.K. (1980) *Hunting and Stalking Deer in Britain through the Ages*. Batsford, London

Tree Management in Historic Parks

Julian Forbes-Laird

Forbes-Laird Arboricultural Consultancy Ltd

Trees are frequently a defining characteristic of historic parks and parkland and there is little need here to explain how and why this came about. However, the planting and landscape management decisions of the past five hundred years or so have bequeathed to contemporary parkland managers a mixed arboricultural legacy: part irreplaceable asset, part millstone.

Tensions frequently arise between mature and over-mature trees, public access, imperatives of biodiversity, restoration/ preservation of historic settings and, above all, limited budgets. Far too often, these tensions lead to unfortunate management decisions to remove trees that could and sometimes should have been retained.

As this paper explained, modern arboriculture can provide various solutions to several commonly recurring problems, which, taken together, now facilitate desirable levels of tree retention.

Topics covered included:

The role of the professional in assessing and managing risks to public safety

Mature and over-mature trees almost always start to disintegrate pre-mortem and the response to this natural phenomenon of many parkland managers falls some way short of what is desirable and responsible. The benefits of a systematised inspection and remediation programme were explained.

Management of historic avenues into senescence

Few if any historic avenues are deliberately retained and managed into senescence, despite this yielding a range of benefits. The options for a retention-based strategy were explored, and guidance given on when replacement is the more appropriate option.

The fallacy of tree removal to restore so-called 'historic settings'

The evolution of parklands frequently leads to historic planting decisions that fly in the face of the original landscape design: in such cases, most parkland historians advocate tree removal to 'restore' the setting. An explanation was given why this approach is often inherently flawed, and an alternative approach outlined that is more appropriate for the 21st century.

Crown restoration of mature and over-mature trees

Specific advice was offered in relation to crown restoration: how to identify whether this is achievable, and how to maximize tree longevity by mimicking naturally occurring growth patterns.

Figure 1: Regrown crown.

The Living Dead - A quantitative study of dead wood in 3 ancient wood pasture sites in Derbyshire (Poster)

Monica Gillespie
High Peak Borough Council

Introduction

Dead wood is not a single uniform substrate it includes fallen wood, dead standing trees and it is also present in living trees as dead branches, decay, cavities and other dysfunctional wood. Ancient wood pasture sites and their associated ancient trees are important dead wood habitats for many specialised species because of their continuity with post-glacial wildwood (Harding & Alexander, 1993 and Kirby *et al*, 1995). Many studies have quantified fallen dead wood and standing dead trees in woodlands and forests (Kirby *et al*, 1998 and Humphrey *et al*, 2003), however there have been few attempts to quantify dead wood in wood pasture sites. Dead wood present in living trees has virtually been ignored in these previous studies.

The study

A study was undertaken to quantify the dead wood habitats of 3 ancient wood pasture sites in Derbyshire. All the sites have a long history of wood pasture management and many ancient trees, but management has varied between the sites in the last 100 years. At Calke Park there has been minimal intervention and dead wood in most areas is left where it falls. At Kedleston Park dead wood has been moved from the main parkland areas to the woodlands, as it is not considered to be compatible with the 18th century ideal of a 'classical landscape'. Intervention at Hardwick Park has been high with dead wood removed and many old oaks felled in the 20th century.

Deadwood was recorded either as fallen dead wood (FDW) or standing dead wood (SDW). FDW on the site was measured using line-intercept sampling. There is no established methodology for measuring SDW in living trees and as such one was designed for this study. Comparison of the results between the sites shows a clear general trend; the volume, spatial distribution and the diversity of dead wood decreased with increasing intervention. SDW is a significant proportion (37.54%) of all dead wood recorded. Notably SDW in living trees recorded as decay, cavities and dysfunctional wood (excluding entirely dead trees and branches) on average accounted for 25.81% of all dead wood.

Comparison of the volume of dead wood with the species richness data for saproxylic invertebrates available for the sites (Alexander 2004 a, b & c) showed a positive relationship. Although this remains statistically unproven the results strongly suggest that increasing intervention has reduced the value of the sites for saproxylic species.

Impact of management of dead wood habitat

It takes around 100 years without intervention for FDW to reach semi-natural levels (Webster & Jenkins, 2005). SDW as decay and cavities in ancient trees reflects management on a much longer timescale than FDW, possibly several centuries. As such, long term planning is required to ensure the continuity of a diversity of habitats.

The past management of the sites has influenced their value for saproxylic species and there is evidence that local extinctions of some species have already occurred as a result, notably at Hardwick (Alexandra, 2004c). Improving the dead wood habitat on all sites could prevent further loss of species.

Management Challenges

Ideally all FDW should be left where it falls and if necessary only moved short distances. On some sites, however, increasing FDW will be dependent on balancing landscape and biodiversity priorities by agreeing zones of minimal intervention in less visible areas. A wider recognition of the ecological as well as cultural heritage of these sites is required to secure their biodiversity value for the future.

Maintaining existing SDW volumes is dependent on the retention and sensitive management of existing ancient and veteran trees to ensure their longevity. Increasing the level of SDW to ensure suitable habitats for species survival is more of a challenge given the timescales involved in the natural development of this habitat. 'Veteranising' trees by initiating premature decay and senility may bridge gaps in the habitat (Key & Ball, 1993 and Fay, 2002).

Protecting threatened species dependent on dead wood also depends upon extending positive management practices beyond the boundaries of these sites, increasing dead wood and protecting ancient and veteran trees in the wider landscape.

References

Alexander, K.N.A. (2004a) *Saproxylic Invertebrate Survey of Calke Park SSSI, Derbyshire*. Unpublished report for English Nature

Alexander, K.N.A. (2004b) *Saproxylic Invertebrate Survey of Kedleston Park, Derbyshire*. Unpublished report for English Nature

Alexander, K.N.A. (2004c) *Saproxylic Invertebrate Survey of Hardwick Park, Derbyshire*. Unpublished report for English Nature

Fay, N. (2002), The Principles of Environmental Arboriculture. *The Arboricultural Journal* **26** (3).213-238

Harding, P.T. and Alexander, K.N.A. (1993) 'The Saproxylic Invertebrates of Historic Parklands: Progress and Problems.' In Kirby, K. J. and Drake, C. M. (eds) *Dead wood Matters: the ecology and conservation of saproxylic invertebrates in Britain*. English Nature, Peterborough

Humphrey, J., Ferris, R. and Quine, C. (eds) (2003) *Biodiversity in Britain's Planted Forests- Results from the Forestry Commission's Biodiversity Assessment Project*. Forestry Commission, Edinburgh

Key, R.S. & Ball, S.G. (1993) 'Positive management for saproxylic invertebrates' In Kirby, K. J. and Drake, C. M. (eds) *Dead wood matters: the ecology and conservation of saproxylic invertebrates in Britain*. English Nature, Peterborough

Kirby, K., Reid, C.M., Thomas, R.C. and Goldsmith, F.B. (1998) 'Preliminary estimates of fallen dead wood and standing dead trees in managed and unmanaged forests in Britain.' *Journal of Applied Ecology*, **35**, 148-155

Kirby, K., Thomas, R.C, Key, R.S., McLean, I.F.G., and Hodgetts, N. (1995) 'Pasture-woodland and its conservation in Britain.' *Biological Journal of the Linnean Society* **56**: 135-153

Webster, C.R. and Jenkins, (2005) 'Coarse woody debris dynamics in the southern Appalachians as affected by topographic position and anthropogenic disturbance history.' *Forest Ecology and Management*, **217(2-3)** 319-330

Stating the obvious: the biodiversity of an open grown tree - from acorn to ancient

Ted Green

ntroduction

Across Europe north of the Mediterranean region, the open grown and often ageing parkland and hedgerow trees in the UK represent an important habitat for much of the biodiversity associated with old trees. Many would argue that old, open grown trees in parklands are an essential component of the Vera landscape -especially the biological continuity over the centuries for both visible and invisible biodiversity that they have provided. An idea is gaining momentum that the UK's single greatest contribution and obligation to the biodiversity of Europe is the conservation of our veteran and ancient trees.

This article, which to many will be merely stating the obvious, is an attempt to illustrate the importance of open grown trees for biodiversity. Originally, it was not the intention to draw comparisons between the two extreme forms of tree, i.e. the open grown form versus the forest form tree of a similar age. However, in preparing the article it became clear that there might be some interesting comparisons to be drawn between the two forms. The challenge has been in the exercise of setting out and describing some of the vast array of habitats provided on and within a single tree that are an integral part of the co-evolutionary relationships.

Clearly, our ancestors discovered the benefits of the open grown tree and the evidence is all around us today in the form of our orchards and fields full of shrub soft fruits. As far back as hunter gatherers, people would have realised that open grown trees and shrubs could produce vastly more fruit than their equivalent in a grove or woodland. Before fruit come flowers and pollen. Has the analysis of pollen diagrams recognised the quantity and mobility of pollen production from an open grown tree compared with the smaller, less productive canopies and reduced mobility of pollen from woodland and close grown trees? This could have a huge effect on the availability of fruit in these landscapes.

The Open Grown Tree

An open grown tree is one that has developed virtually all its life without competition from other trees. It has a short, squat, fat trunk with very large diameter, spreading limbs of which some grow out almost horizontally. They have a large dome-like canopy compared with a forest form tree that is tall with a narrow trunk and a small canopy. The forest form tree may often have the remains of dead limbs below the canopy that have died through competition for light either from limbs above or neighbouring trees. Therefore, an open grown tree compared with a tree of similar age growing in confined woodland conditions will have a far greater diversity of organisms and a greater biomass production. Whilst the mass and diversity per unit area of canopy in woodland might in many instances be very similar, the production of leaves and roots will be far greater in the open grown form. The volume of wood in the trunk of a forest form tree might be greater than the trunk of an open grown tree of the same age but the open grown tree also has considerable timber in its large spreading limbs.

The dome of an open grown tree is perhaps the most efficient shape for collecting energy and the greater the leaf area the greater the photosynthesis. The root system below ground must equate proportionately to the canopy above ground. An open grown tree has little or no competition, whereas woodland trees face constant stress from neighbours and consequently have shorter lives. The former may therefore be productive and therefore providing habitat for as much as several centuries longer.

Underground it is very difficult to assess the extent and volume of any individual root system. However, there are some examples to be found. The Ancient Tree Forum traced roots from an ancient open grown oak in a recently cultivated and destroyed ancient grassland sward on a National Trust property. The roots were still 2.5 cm in diameter over 50m from the trunk of the tree. There are also good examples showing the extent of exposed roots; beech trees that are growing on steep banks along old sunken lanes or quarries; granny pines on eroded river banks and hillsides; and ash appears to regularly produce extremely large diameter roots several metres in length just on the surface. Often the area covered and volume of these roots is far greater than the canopy.

In addition, one needs to take account of mycorrhizal associations. They may extend over very large areas and can be interconnected with other trees and even different species of trees and plants. These complex relationships can be ever changing and are now increasingly being recognised for their importance in natural ecosystems. Perhaps a tree's roots can be likened to an inverted, much flattened tree. The 'branches, twigs and leaves' of the root system expand and then contract with age, probably in direct correlation with the canopy. It appears that subterranean dead roots can have a distinct decay (recycling) ecosystem.

The Forest Grown Tree

Forest form trees growing in close competition with small canopies are still capable of gathering sufficient energy to produce often large volumes of wood in the trunk. However, trees on the margin with a greater leaf area may be able to provide extra energy to their neighbours on the inside of the group via their grafted roots.

In dense beech woodland or groves, presumably there are more trees, greater density and competition, and the greater the progressive

self-thinning. There will be more production of dead wood, and the recycling of minerals and nutrients from the decaying wood. There is a constant supply of nutrients to the survivors through this recycling. By having a very efficient, co-evolutionary, micro-organism support system it may be the trees only require a relatively small root area especially feeder roots. Individual trees do not require large spreading buttress roots as they are growing in dense tight conditions. They give each other group support against the elements reducing the need for each tree to adapt individually to wind exposure. However there is intense competition for space for other trees and plant roots to colonise in these far more restricted dense grove conditions.

It is generally accepted that open grown trees develop substantial buttress roots in response to continual exposure to wind. It will therefore have a greater number, diversity, and mass of micro-organisms associated with the roots simply through the greater area available to individual species to colonise the roots.

The length of the decay cycle will be far shorter in the more humid conditions found in woodlands and groves. A mature fallen beech with a trunk diameter of 1m could well disappear back into the woodland soil within 30-40 years. However, a large fallen oak limb of about 60cms diameter in open conditions might still be present after 50-100 years. Therefore, the time-lapse of decomposition of live wood to dead wood ratio is far shorter in woodland compared with open grown trees. Regardless of whether it is ripewood or heartwood it will decay more quickly in woodland.

Hollowing of trees is now widely accepted as a perfectly natural function in non-living wood of most plants including palms. It is usually associated with the ageing process. In deciduous trees, the non -living wood is either heartwood or ripewood that can be decayed by many species of fungi that may be associated with other micro-organisms in the decay process. There are circumstances where some species of saproxylic beetle and other insects including tree ants, may also play important roles. The decay of non-living wood in the centre of trees can be an added benefit to the tree by releasing nutrients locked up in the heart- or ripewood. For example, hollow trees and what they contain in the rainforests, are very important for retaining nutrients that otherwise would be leached away through high rainfall. A succession of different organisms will benefit from different size cavities created by the progress of hollowing.

Conclusions

The biodiversity of the decay (recycling) system is extremely complex and poorly understood. The diversity of species both visible and invisible that carry out essential roles and comprise the major players - '*the bio-engine of recycling*', can only be speculated on. We know it would include bacteria, fungi, invertebrates (of which nematodes must be singled out for their importance) and presumably any single organism could be the primary coloniser which might then facilitate an ever changing succession of other micro-organisms. All these organisms will provide food for other organisms. The fruit bodies produced by fungi are an interesting example. The soft fleshy annual mushrooms usually appear from the end of summer through the autumn and into early winter. Not only are they a source of food for animals including man, slugs, several species of insects (beetles and flies) and nematodes. The insects, often flies, are emerging from the fruit bodies at the time when the bulk of other insects are finished for the year. Therefore, they provide a succession of food especially for birds, bats, and small rodents at a period when other insect food is declining. Other fungal fruit bodies that have a woody texture are usually perennial and associated with decaying wood and do not necessarily produce adult insects in the autumn months. The wholesale picking of fruit bodies not only for commercial reasons but also for the pot by eastern Europeans is on the increase. The impact of this continual loss on the woodland ecosystem appears to be totally lost on so-called ecologists.

Trees annually produce plant matter that eventually dies and decomposes, and is recycled into the system. The biodiversity of this recycling system is diverse, extremely complex, ever changing, and poorly understood. It includes the biodiversity associated with the following:

- The plant matter that is regularly produced and recycled (annually or biannually) includes: leaves, bud cases, some small twigs, flowers and catkins, fruits, fruit cases, and the outer bark of some tree species

- Other plant matter that eventually dies on a regular basis as part of the normal ageing process or at times of stress includes: bark, limbs, trunk, buttress roots, and roots

- The hollowing process as living sapwood in the limbs, trunk, and buttress roots becomes dysfunctional and the heartwood/ripewood centre decays

It has been a very thought provoking exercise to try to encapsulate the differences between open grown and forest form trees over time. It has thrown up more questions than answers.

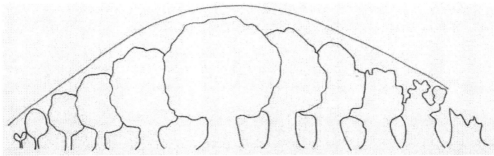

Figure 1. Sequential changes of the canopy area and trunk girth of an individual open grown oak. Overall time span could be up to 500 years and frequently up to 1000 years.

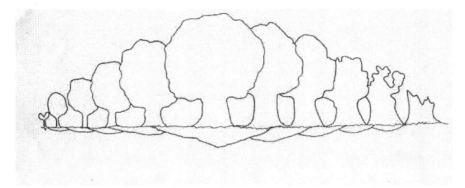

Figure 2: Sequential changes in the root area in relation to crown area of an individual open grown oak

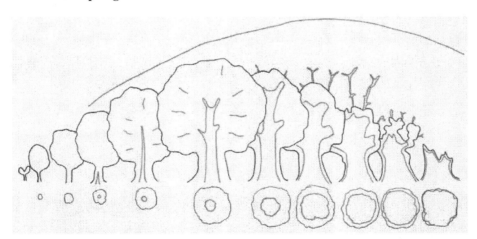

Figure 3. Sequential changes to the deadwood and hollowing of an individual open grown oak "A supply of successional, structural, sustainable decaying wood from acorn to ancient"

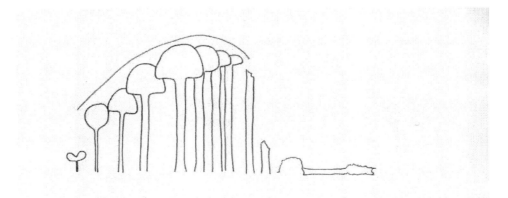

Figure 4. Sequential changes of the canopy area and trunk girth of forest form trees. Overall time span in the case of oak could be less than 400 years and in the case of beech between 200-300 years

Figure 5. Sequential changes in the root area in relation to crown area of forest form trees

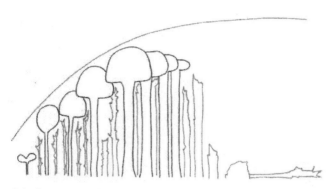

Figure 6. Sequential changes to deadwood from self-thinning of dense forest form trees

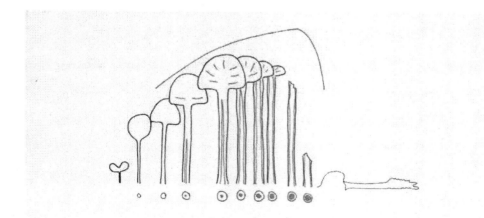

Figure 7. Sequential changes to the hollowing of forest form trees

Chillingham Wild Cattle Park, Northumberland

Stephen J.G. Hall

Department of Biological Sciences, University of Lincoln

Abstract

Chillingham Park, Northumberland has been, for an indeterminate period, the home of the Chillingham Wild White Cattle. Its medieval history is obscure. From 1799, it was developed, following the design of the estate steward, John Bailey, as a 1,500-acre park explicitly for the maintenance of the cattle, with fallow and red deer. The design has been successful in that the herd has continued to survive into the twenty-first century.

Introduction

Chillingham Park, Northumberland is a Georgian park superimposed on earlier layouts and designed by the estate steward, John Bailey (1750-1819) to ensure a habitat for fallow deer, red deer and free-ranging wild cattle. The design took full account of agronomic realities in that it also provided for the production of winter feed, without which only a small and extinction-prone herd could have been maintained.

The development of Chillingham Park has had three phases. In 1711, it comprised the inner park of about 100 acres, adjacent to the castle and including previously tilled land, separated by a wall from the outer park, also enclosed by a wall, within which was the Great Wood of Chillingham. These walls were realigned, the Great Wood was felled, and new plantations made on the more upland areas, from 1754. From 1799, the park was extended over the parish boundary and around to the south and west. The new outer wall enclosed about 1,500 acres. In Victorian times, land previously part of the inner park was planted up, together with other land from the 1799 addition, to create high woodlands including exotic conifers around Chillingham castle. From 1914, the area available to the cattle was progressively reduced. Conifer afforestation of the peripheral north and east areas took place during the 1960s.

The Chillingham Wild White Cattle

Recent reports on the management of the herd are given by Hall et al. (2005) and by Hall (2006). The origin of these cattle is unknown. Genetic studies have confirmed the history of inbreeding (Visscher et al., 2001) but have not, so far, established clear links with any other breed of cattle. The small body size and the general conformation might indicate they are a medieval relict. Skeletal studies, which have concentrated on cranial and dental features (Bilton, 1957; Grigson, 1974; Ingham, 2002), have not cast light on breed affinities either.

Landscape history of Chillingham Park

Since the late eighteenth century, with the description of the Chillingham Wild Cattle in Bewick's *Quadrupeds* (Bewick, 1790; Jessop & Boyd, 1996), the significance of Chillingham Park in the public mind resided in its being the home of the wild cattle.

Chillingham Castle, Chillingham Home Farm, Chillingham Park and the herd of wild white cattle all used to be the property of the Earls of Tankerville but are now owned by three separate entities. Chillingham Castle and the part of Chillingham Park closest to the Castle are in private ownership, as is Chillingham Home Farm, part of which comprises fields formerly in Chillingham Park. The Chillingham Wild Cattle Association owns the herd, the rest of the Park and some adjoining woodlands. However, the coherence of the landscape has not been irremediably altered by these developments.

Chillingham Park ranges in altitude from 88m to 315m above sea level. Its aspect is WSW and it faces the Cheviot (815m asl) which is approximately 17km away across the Till valley. Immediately to the east and sharing the summit of Ros Castle is an Iron Age encampment (owned by the National Trust), a noted viewpoint (315m asl).

The earliest cartographic depiction of Chillingham Park is the Chillingham estate terrier drawn in 1711 and now in the possession of the Northumberland Record Office. The early history of Chillingham Park is summarised by Dodds (1935) who presented a map of the Park made by the steward John Bailey in 1799. This depicts proposed extensions, a plan which was superseded by subsequent land purchases.

Key dates in this history, taken from Dodds (1935) or from documents in the NRO or PRO are as follows:

1629 - William Lord Grey of Chillingham obtained licence "to enclose and make into a Park their lands containing about forty acres enclosed with walls called Chillingham Parke adjoining the site of ... Chillingham Castle ...; and to enclose as much as they will of the land ... not exceeding in all, 1,500 acres ...". This could have regularised an earlier enclosure.

1645-46 - Earliest written record of the wild cattle: "What with the Soldiers, and this continuing Storme if it lye but one Month more, there will bee neither Beast nor Sheepe left in the Country. Your Honour's Deere and wild Cattle, I fear will all dye, doe what wee can: The lik of this storme hath not beene knowne by any living in the Country ...".

1711 - Estate terrier prepared by Henry Pratt of London. The boundaries depicted here probably date back at least to 1629, but it has been claimed that the park was established when the castle was crenellated in 1344, i.e. some boundaries could date back to then, or even earlier.

1721 - The steward at Chillingham was William Browne (who was 73 years old "and every day growing more and more infirm"). In a letter of May 4 to Earl of Tankerville - "The Great Park & Wood I have not valued your L^{dps} Stock there being sufficient to Depasture the whole (there being a large stock of Deer and 27 or thereabouts of Wild Cattle with some Horses of your L^{dps} that may happen to be there and the Park Keepers Cows & Horses. I have put a value upon the Inner Park but believing it will be impossible to find out a way to hinder the Deer coming into it without your Lordship should raise a High Wall to keep them in with will require a good round Sum to finish it." The Great Wood covered 192 acres.

1721 - Letter to Mr. Browne "... as for the Great Park his Lordship does intend to Dispark and turn it to a more advantageous purpose designing to keep only a few Deer ...". However, Mr. Browne took a 21-year lease of Outer & Inner Parks and other lands, but not the Great Wood. Earl is to "make the inner dike fencible to keep the Deer & wild Beasts within the bounds of the Upper Park ...". This letter also mentions the winter hay feeding of the deer and wild cattle.

1722 - Second Earl dies. Order sent to Mr. Browne - "This is to Desire you will Deliver to Mr. Edward Ward of Morpeth or to his Order All the Horses & Live Cattle belonging to the Right Honble Charles late Earl of Tankerville ...".

Reply -

"you have on ye Back syde of the Inventory the other part of my late Lords personall estate ... I presum'd the White Cattle in ye Park will not be put into it they being ferae natura ...".

1753 - Third Earl succeeded - Great Wood felled 1755-1759 for timber, for around £4,000, a price which disappointed Jos. Hutchinson the current steward who had asked for 4,000 guineas. The letters are not fully legible but it seems that the trees were "very old & shaken, great Loss will attend it". Contracts were let to build a new wall using the old stones. The new wall was built around the Inner Park. Completed October 1754. Hutchinson "gave the Masons a supper & Drink".

The Outer Park appears to have been left alone. One might surmise that the boundary wall marked on the 1711 terrier was repaired and upgraded. Mr. Hutchinson wrote on 1 March 1754: "I have scratcht out a Rough Plan of the Park, in which is most Sorts of Land and that will grow all Sorts of Trees of English Produce - the outer Park is such Rough Land with Wood, Roots, Stones, Haddor & Juniper Bushes, that it will cost a great deal to make it Plowable ...".

1784 or 1785 - John Bailey becomes steward at Chillingham (*Dictionary of National Biography*: mathematician, agriculturist and land surveyor, also painter and engraver, and co-author of the county agricultural survey - Bailey & Culley, 1797).

1788 - "Robin Hood's Boggs" planted. This is the 20-hectare alder, oak and beech woodland at the NE of the park, to which the cattle have full access to this day. At least one ancient oak in the area probably pre-dates this plantation.

1789 - 11th January Chillingham Old Park mentioned as a farm tenanted by James Scott.

1799 - Bailey tells Earl that there were 48 cattle & 150 deer on 100 acres, i.e. the Inner Park established by Hutchinson. Previously there had been about 30 cattle. Earl instructs him to enlarge the Park.

1799 - Bailey describes the proposed extension thus - "and altogether will make a noble Park and include a great variety of Ground - the heathery Moor wd. be a considerable acquisition - and in its present state it is of very little value".

1800 - cattle & deer to be kept in outer Park May- December; inner Park to grow hay.

1801 - took possession of 450 acres of the Old Park, cattle put in.

1803 - 1st September Bailey writes - "Your Lordship expresses a fear that the ground in coming in, looks ill since the hedges were removed. It is now making the worst appearance it will ever do as from the great drought, the grass seeds that were soon on the foundations of the old hedges have not grown well, and there are too many Thorns and Trees left which mark the old inclosures too conspicuously but these were purposely left to be taken out afterwards according as might be judged most proper, for giving a Park like effect, as Trees and bushes can be much easier taken out than put in: when some alterations of this kind are made I think it will look very well, but there is a great deal of this kind to do yet - in every part of the Park ...".

1803 - 5th March to Lady Tankerville - "We were going on very fast with the planting but the frost and snow has put a stop to it the old hedges and earth mounds are nearly all thrown down - and we shall begin to take away the present park wall as soon as the land is sufficiently dry to carry the carts".

c1800 - possibility arises of purchasing part or all of Hebburn estate (the neighbouring parish to the south). Negotiations proceeded over the next few years.

1808 - wall finally completed adding the "Hebburn lands"; public road realigned. This extended the Park over the parish boundary.

Partitioning within the new (1799-1810) park wall proceeded, and Bailey's later letters report on hacking up roads and removing old stone walls, constructing "Broad Conduits over the Burns and Rills", "railing off the Hay Grounds", cutting drains (7,700 yards) and other works. The final pattern of partitioning was presumably that marked on the 1860 OS 1:2500 map.

Probable inspiration for Bailey's landscape design

The studies by Thomas Bewick in 1789, and his friend John Bailey, dated 1794 (illustrated by Jessop & Boyd, 1996) present the animals as being at home in a very well-wooded landscape. In the former case, the trees are clean-stemmed with possibly oak in the foreground and beech in the background. In the latter, the trees show many dead limbs and a conformation that strongly implies that they are alders.

With the Great Wood having been felled by 1760, and Robin Hood's Boggs only just having been planted, the mature trees illustrated by Bewick must have been the product of artistic licence. In contrast, streamside alders such as in Bailey's depiction were abundant, alder stools over 200 years old abound in the Park today.

It is contended that these views represent the ideal to which Bailey aspired in his planning of the 1799 park. The Park was designed by Bailey to be a dramatic backcloth to the lives of the cattle. The grassy meadows provided grazing and the woods the ancestral fastnesses, while the hayfields were necessary for the winter grazing which was vital for a reasonably sized herd. He was re-creating what was thought to be the pristine woodland environment of the herd's supposedly direct forebears.

The trackways around the Park, depicted in the 1860 map, do not provide planned routes around the Park. They radiate from the Deer Hemmel in the centre, rather than from the natural points of entry for visitors and castle residents. These tracks are fully explicable as providing routes into the better-drained low-lying areas for hay carts in winter.

The landscape today is very similar to that conceived by Bailey in 1799. Differences are as follows: today there exist the plantation between the Deer Hemmel and the lake in the dell near the Castle; the lake itself; the exotic conifers around the Castle; the Victorian alterations to the castle and gardens; modern cropping patterns in the fields removed from the Park in the twentieth century.

As a progressive agriculturist Bailey would have approved of the dense twentieth century planting of conifers (mainly Scots pine) at Chillingham, though his preference was for larch (Bailey & Culley, 1797, p. 109). He would have deplored the prevalence of bracken and the impeded drainage evident two hundred years after his stewardship.

The redesigns of the park in both 1754 and 1799 were carried out by the stewards of the time, Joseph Hutchinson and John Bailey respectively. Regarding more famous landscape architects, there is no record of Capability Brown (1715 / 16-1783) or of his well-known successors, having worked at Chillingham, nor evidence of his influence.

The consequences for the cattle

During the nineteenth century, the Chillingham wild cattle and the other park herds became famous and romanticized members of the British fauna (Whitehead, 1953; Hall & Clutton-Brock, 1988). The resources of the Park made it possible to maintain the herd at an average of 61 animals (minimum 49, maximum 73) between 1862 and 1899 (Hall & Hall, 1988) with 40 red deer and 300-400 fallow deer. Under financial pressure in the twentieth century, the area of the Park accessible to the cattle was reduced. The red deer were wiped out soon after 1900, and the cattle herd halved in size by culling, down to 40 head in 1918. The reduced grazing area, coupled with bad winter weather (notably in 1947), increased stocking rate of sheep, and other factors, has probably caused the lower, and fluctuating, population sizes in the late twentieth century.

Current management

The management priority has been the maintenance of the herd, though further research on the landscape, on the trees, and on the pasture plant communities is proceeding. The Park is now subject to a management plan agreed with Defra as part of Higher Level Environmental Stewardship. A survey of ground archaeological features was made during early 2007 and is yet to be reported.

Acknowledgements

This study would not have been possible without the interest, hospitality, and generosity of the late Violet, Dowager Countess of Tankerville, and the late Hon. Ian Bennet. Financial support during archival research came from the Animal Health Trust, Newmarket, in the form of a Wooldridge Farm Livestock Research Fellowship.

References

Bailey, J. & Culley, G. (1797) *General View of the Agriculture of the County of Northumberland with Observations on the Means of its Improvement*. Newcastle-upon-Tyne, Hodgson

Bewick, T. (1790) *A General History of Quadrupeds*. Newcastle-upon-Tyne, Edward Walker

Bilton, L. (1957) The Chillingham Herd of Wild Cattle. *Transactions of the Natural History Society of Northumberland, Durham and Newcastle-upon-Tyne* (new series), **12**, 137-160

Dodds, M.H. (1935) Chillingham Parish. Area and Population, in Dodds, M.H. (Ed.): A history of Northumberland. *Victoria County History*, **Vol. XIV**, Newcastle-upon-Tyne, Andrew Reid

Grigson, C. (1974) The Craniology and Relationships of Four Species of Bos 1. Basic Craniology: Bos taurus L. and its Absolute Size. *Journal of Archaeological Science*, **1**, 353-379

Hall, S.J.G. (2006) Chillingham Park and its Wild White Cattle. *Journal of the Royal Agricultural Society of England*, **167**, 40-48

Hall, S.J.G., & Clutton-Brock, J. (1988) *Two Hundred Years of British Farm Livestock*. British Museum Natural History, London

Hall, S. J. G., Hall, J. G. (1988) Inbreeding and Population Dynamics of the Chillingham Cattle (Bos taurus). *Journal of Zoology*, London, **216**, 479-493

Hall, S.J.G., Fletcher, T.J., Gidlow, J.R., Ingham, B., Shepherd, A., Smith, A., & Widdows, A. (2005) Management of the Chillingham Wild Cattle. *Government Veterinary Journal*, **15**, 4-11

Ingham, B. (2002) Dental Anomalies in the Chillingham Wild White Cattle. *Transactions of the Natural History Society of Northumbria*, **62**, 169-175

Jessop, L., & Boyd, M.J. (1996) Some Sources for Thomas Bewick's Work on the Chillingham "Wild" Cattle. *Transactions of the Natural History Society of Northumbria*, **57**, 21-34

Visscher, P.M., Smith, D., Hall, S.J.G., & Williams, J.A. (2001) A Viable Herd of Genetically Uniform Cattle. *Nature*, London, **409**, 303

Whitehead, G.K. (1953) *The Ancient White Cattle of Britain and their Descendants*. Faber and Faber, London

Saproxylic beetle survey of Richmond Park 2005-7 (Poster)

Peter M. Hammond[1] & Nigel J. Reeve[2]

[1] 33 St Marks Road, Windsor, Berks, SL4 3BD. [2] Roehampton University

Introduction

Richmond Park (South West London) encloses almost 1,000 hectares of historic parkland. Famous for its varied landscape and deer herds, it is one of the UK's top sites for veteran trees with 1,387 ancient trees of fourteen species, including about 954 ancient English oaks. The Park is London's largest Site of Special Scientific Interest (SSSI), a National Nature Reserve (NNR), and a European Special Area for Conservation (SAC). Richmond Park is important for a number of habitat types and their associated flora and fauna, but among these are more than 1,350 species of beetle. When designated in 1992, the Park's community of over 200 saproxylic beetle species was recognised as internationally significant. The Park has since become well known in the general biodiversity and conservation biology literature (e.g. Gaston *et al.*, 1993; Hammond, 1992, 1994, 1995; Stork & Hammond, 1997; Stork *et al.*, 2001). Nevertheless, this study is the first systematic re-survey of saproxylic species since the Park's designation.

The present study

The present study began in autumn 2005, with a review of beetle records for the site and seven field visits with direct hand-gathering from rot holes (mainly in English oak and beech) around most of the Park. This preliminary work was followed up by placing Perspex vane traps in thirty veteran English oaks in five areas of the Park (five traps per area) plus five traps in selected individual trees. Sample bottles (containing 70% ethanol) were changed fortnightly from 2nd May to 28th November 2006. All traps were closed for repair and modification for two weeks (19th September to 3rd October). Only eighteen traps were used

from 3rd October onwards but all five trapping areas were represented. In total, 365 trap samples were collected over seven months.

Results

The site list of saproxylic beetles now stands at 347 species, with the winter 2005-6 survey adding seventeen new records, and the vane traps in 2006 adding a further twenty-nine species new to the Park. Of the total, 138 have conservation status as either notable or Red Data Book (RDB). (9 RDB1, 4 RDB2, 11 RDB3, 4 RDBI, 6 RDBK, 104 Notable).

Discussion

For site evaluation, hand searching by a specialist provides key data, additional to those obtained only by trapping. However, vane trapping is highly productive and seems to be the best current option for standardised sampling and inter-site comparisons. The results reaffirm the importance of Richmond Park as a top site for saproxylic beetles. New data for *Trinodes hirtus* (RDB3), *Ampedus cardinalis* (RDB2), and *Procraerus tibialis* (RDB3) show that these very rare species remain well established in the Park. Some of the more notable newly recorded species include *Cryptophagus falcozi* (RDB1), *Ischnomera caerulea* (RDB3) and a 'Windsor' weevil *Dryophthorus corticalis* (RDB1) was trapped in the 27th June-10th July 2006 period. In recent times, since it was found there in 1925, Windsor Great Park has been the only UK site for this beetle. This discovery in Richmond Park, plus a find (by PMH) in 2006 in Langley Park (Buckinghamshire), may represent additional relict populations or result from recent dispersals from Windsor. Also of interest is the apparent absence of some species that, although not common, are found on other

Ampedus cardinalis 17 Dec 2005 © Nigel Reeve

**Veteran oaks with dead wood, Richmond Park ©
Nigel Reeve**

suitable sites. Further work is needed in order
to understand the reasons for such inter-site
differences, as well as further work on the other
non-beetle taxa in the vane trap samples.

Acknowledgements

This study was supported by funding from The
Friends of Richmond Park and help from the
beetle survey volunteers, especially John Hatto.
The City of London (thanks to Jeremy Dagley
& Imogen Wilde) provided traps. Thanks to
Royal Parks staff especially Jo Scrivener, Adam
Curtis, Simon Richards (Park Manager) and
Mike Turner. Samantha Wilkinson helped with
fieldwork and sorted more than half the
samples. Thanks also to the tree contractors
(The Tree Company) and to Philippa Richards
and Clare Bowen who each spent a day sorting
samples.

References

Gaston, K.J., Blackburn, T.M., Hammond, P.M.
& Stork, N.E. (1993) Relationships between
abundance and body size: where do tourists fit?
Ecological Entomology, **18**, 310-314

Hammond, P.M. (1992) Species Inventory. In:
Groombridge, B. (Ed.) *Global biodiversity:
status of the Earth's living resources*. Chapman
& Hall, London, pp. 17-39

Hammond, P.M. (1994) Practical approaches to
the estimation of the extent of biodiversity of
speciose groups. *Philosophical Transactions of
the Royal Society of London*, **B 345**, 119-136

Hammond, P.M. (1995) *The current magnitude
of biodiversity*. In: Heywood, V. (Ed.) *Global
Biodiversity Assessment*. Cambridge University
Press, Cambridge, pp. 113-138

Stork, N.E. & Hammond, P.M. (1997) *Sampling
arthropods from tree-crowns by fogging with
knockdown insecticides: lessons from studies of
oak tree beetle assemblages in Richmond Park
(U.K.)*. In: Stork, N.E., Adis, J. &. Didham,
R.K (Eds.) *Canopy arthropods*. Chapman &
Hall, London, pp. 3-26

Stork, N.E., Hammond, P.M., Russell, B.L. &
Hadwen, W.L. (2001) The spatial distribution
of beetles within the canopies of oak trees in
Richmond Park, U.K. *Ecological Entomology*,
26, 302-311

An historic and archaeological survey of Cornish deer and ornamental parks

Peter Herring

Introduction

Deer parks can reveal more than might be expected about medieval life. They were among the earliest restricted outdoor spaces and were often created at the expense of tenants' homes, fields, and rights. Through this and their association with established symbols of contemporary and former power (churches, hillforts, *etc*), they made the unequal power relations of feudal society concrete and permanently visible. Careful study of the location, shape, and topography of a number of Cornish parks indicates that they also involved sophisticated landscape design, suggesting they were close ancestors of the better-known ornamental parks of the eighteenth and nineteenth centuries. Some of this design served to reinforce further the status of those laying out the parks.

A recent survey of Cornish deer parks recorded 123, of which forty-nine are certainly medieval, and a further twenty-six probably are. Some may be as early as the late twelfth century. Most can be located, and around twenty survive sufficiently well for their circuits to be plotted with confidence. (See Herring 2003 for fully referenced report, of which this paper is a summary).

The best-preserved parks are in rough ground where there has been least post-medieval disturbance. However, it becomes clear from correlating the sites of parks with the Cornwall historic landscape characterisation (HLC), that they were not normally placed on the less valuable rough ground on the edges of estates as some writers have thought. Instead, they were usually established in the agricultural heartland, the *Anciently Enclosed Land*. Indeed many parks either surrounded or were immediately adjacent to the house or castle to which they belonged. Continuous agricultural activity in the 400 or 500 years since most parks were closed, explains why so few survive in a reasonable condition. Those who set parks in rough ground appear on closer examination to have done so to obtain particular landscape effects.

HLC can also be used to estimate that most Cornish parks would have typically comprised around 25% woodland, the remainder being a mix of open grassland and rough ground. There is some confirmation of this proportion of woodland in medieval records.

Shapes of parks varied; they might be nicely sub-circular or sub-ovoid where the country was open (either rough ground or subdivided fields). However, where enclosure of strip fields had already begun (quite common by the fourteenth century in Cornwall) the parks often had irregular shapes to accommodate the existing built hedges. Cornish parks also varied in size, from the pocket parks attached to the Earldom of Cornwall castles at Launceston and Trematon (both under 50 acres) and the small parks at Bennacott (*c.* 62 acres) and Pengersick (*c.* 26.5 acres), to the very large parks which appear to have been sufficiently extensive for hunting to take place. These included Liskeard New Park (580 acres), Restormel (549 acres), Kerrybullock (465 acres), and Godolphin (over 400 acres).

Evidence

All the documentary and archaeological evidence from Cornwall suggests that the animals contained were fallow deer, the favourite for sport. The males (harts or bucks) were probably killed from June to mid September when they were fattening for the autumnal rut and the females (hinds or does) in winter (late November to mid-February). It is likely that much of the killing was done to order by servants, to provide the high-status venison that was either eaten at table (fresh or salted) or sent as gifts to those the lord wished to influence. However, some deer were taken as sport. There are clear documentary records of chases within Restormel Park in the fourteenth century and it may be assumed that the other large Cornish parks were also so used. Later medieval or early post-medieval means of dispatching deer may be represented by features and structures at Godolphin. Raised walks projecting into the park may have been used as 'stables' from which driven deer were shot, and there is also evidence for a short deer course at Godolphin along which a single young male deer, or pricket, would have been chased by two or more greyhounds. Bets were laid on which dog would be the first to cross a finishing line marked by a viewing stand at the end of the course.

The Parks in the Landscape

The undulating and dissected topography of Cornwall makes it relatively easy to identify landscape design. At the simplest level of analysis, medieval deer parks were set so that they were either effectively secluded and private, or open to view or on display. Closer examination of those parks that survive relatively well reveals more subtle design than this.

The Cardinans were among Cornwall's most substantial twelfth century families and they created at Cardinham, Restormel and Penhallam three very similar, but otherwise unusual parks. Their similarity suggests they were working to a common design. In each, the pale was run just beyond the crest of the sides of a central valley so that on the one hand few could look into the park and on the other, and perhaps most significantly, those on the inside could see very little of the world beyond the park. The effect the huntsman experienced was that the Cardinan parks ran on forever and were dream-like chases or forests. The one at Restormel had the roughly centrally placed castle (now an English Heritage Guardianship Site) coming in and out of view as the chase ran in and out of the side valleys.

However, the Cardinan parks also benefited from an additional quality that those earlier, open and more extensive forms of hunting grounds, the forests and chases, lacked. They were unencumbered with sight or sound of peasants and of the ordinary or mundane. What was cunningly contrived here, were pure hunting landscapes. This suggests that medieval Cornish people (and presumably others elsewhere in Britain) were aware of the idea or concept of landscape. Others have demonstrated how the surroundings of castles and towns, and approaches to them, have been equally well designed. We can easily imagine how power relations could have been reinforced through such devices (see below for an example at Launceston).

In contrast to the subtle Cardinans, the Bassets of Tehidy established their deer park to include the summit of Carn Brea, the most dramatic tor-topped hill in Kerrier. As well as taking from their tenants a large portion of their common grazing and fuel grounds, they displayed for all to see, the replacement of sheep by deer, an animal without wool and whose flesh the peasant could not eat. To emphasise further the Bassets' status, they also erected an eye-catching mini-castle (probably really a hunting lodge) on one of the tors. Moreover, as if to confirm to future archaeologists what their intentions were, they ran their park pale around only those two tors (out of three), that could be seen from their home at Tehidy. The park at Godolphin worked in a similar way to that at Carn Brea. It may be significant here that the Godolghan family was newly established in Cornish society; their highly visible deer park a flag seen from miles away.

Consideration of how Launceston deer park, established by the most powerful person in mid-thirteenth century Cornwall, Richard Earl of Cornwall, worked reveals other forms of medieval landscape design. These are similar to examples previously identified by Paul Everson at Ludgershall in Wiltshire, and by Rob Liddiard at Castle Rising in Norfolk. Both revolved around carefully controlled approaches to castles.

Earl Richard was clearly aware of the power of place and at Launceston established a very effective place of power. Roads guided travellers to and through two of its key elements, a walled and gated town, and the bailey of the Norman castle, which he had enhanced through the construction of a great hall, and a high tower within the drum of the motte's shell keep. The deer park, to one side of the sloping bailey, helped control access to the new barbicanned south gateway to the castle; the new town wall formed the other side of a funnel down which all visitors from the west, from Cornwall itself, were obliged to flow. The road itself was well placed in a valley from which there were no direct views of the castle and then run alongside the park pale as it climbed eastwards towards the castle, so that all travellers eventually reached the point where the road levelled and the motte and its bright new high tower suddenly popped up directly ahead. It is still possible to be awe-struck by the effect in modern traffic-dominated Launceston; imagine how the effect would have worked on those whom the Earl was trying to impress.

Once within the bailey, the motte, and the curtain walls blocked views into the town and farmland to the north and south. The deer park was carefully positioned to dominate the foreground of the longest westward views from the bailey. The only large first floor window in the high tower also looks out across the park.

Deer parks were very expensive to create (external pales, compartmental pales, gates, lodge, deer shelters, feeding racks, *etc*), and to maintain. Most also involved a loss of revenue (the returns from agistment and occasional timber sales falling short of the rental income foregone) and at Godolphin even involved the sterilisation of a potentially rich tin lode which was isolated by the park. John Hatcher, having studied their accounts, considered the Earldom and then Duchy of Cornwall deer parks to have been an 'expensive and rather unnecessary luxury' and thought their disparking by Henry VIII 'a sensible economy'. However, this rationalisation occurred nearly two centuries after the last Duke to have hunted in a Cornish

park had visited Cornwall (Edward the Black Prince in 1376). While Hatcher's utilitarian attitude to parks seems sound to an economist, it does not explain why dozens of other lesser lords than the Earls and Dukes felt the need to spend large sums on establishing and maintaining parks. They clearly served other less tangible but clearly important purposes. One of these may have been simply to give aesthetic, sensory, and sporting pleasure to the hunters, the family themselves, but also others the family had an interest in influencing. Although most of the larger Cornish parks were not as neatly designed as the Cardinan family's, they all worked as contained hunting arenas within which the ordinary and mundane would not be encountered, and which had attractive mixes of land cover. The latter included meadow, rough ground and wooded cover, and usually including areas of wood pasture dotted with large oaks.

Cornwall's Park and the Community

Another way of approaching the meaning of deer parks is to consider how others responded to them. The most common form of medieval reference to deer parks in Cornwall is through formal complaints or actions against 'breakers', those who entered and stole one or more deer. Again the details that emerge from the Cornish records may be surprising, but they are certainly revealing of the ways that parks served as symbols of their owners. Breaks against smaller private parks were often done not by starving peasants, but by people who may be regarded as the owner's peers. The Basset's Carn Brea Park was broken by two other landowners from the same part of Cornwall, John de Lambourn and Reginald de Bevyle, presumably happy to be identified as those who cocked a snook at their rather grander neighbour.

It may be more surprising to see how the medieval clergy behaved. Some of Cornwall's most substantial parks belonged to the Bishop of Exeter, and these too were occasionally broken. That at Pawton was broken in 1301, by Walter, the rector of Boconnoc, a parish that possibly already contained its famous park. He would have passed several other parks on his way to Pawton so his motives seem to have been less to obtain venison and more to make a statement against the Bishop. At the Bishop's park at Penryn the perpetrators of breaks later in the fourteenth century were the canons of nearby Glasney College who gained access to the park through their postern doors; their depredations were so great that they were eventually threatened with excommunication.

The Earldom, and then from 1337 the Duchy of Cornwall, was in effect the English crown represented in Cornwall, the Duke being the monarch's eldest son. Breaking their parks may have been particularly symbolic, and it is of interest that most of the numerous breaks recorded in the late thirteenth and early fourteenth centuries were by people who were not identified. Were these disaffected individuals striking against the crown? What suggests that they might have been is the case in 1343, when the names were given of those individuals accused, amongst other actions taken against the Duke's interests, of breaking four Duchy parks - Liskeard, Kerrybullock, Restormel and Trematon. It seems that most of Cornish society was involved in a form of concerted campaign against the Duchy: the Bishop of Exeter, the Priors of St Michael's Mount, Bodmin, Launceston and Tywardreath, the Dean of St Buryan, four knights and a further forty-five named people as well as 'others'.

We begin to appreciate what deer parks meant for lord, bishop, and priest. Power was reinforced at some parks by their association with former symbols of authority: prehistoric forts at Carn Brea, Lanner, Swannacott and Tremayne, contemporary parish churches at Lanteglos, Carn Brea (Redruth), Lesnewth and Launcells.

What parks meant for peasants was probably very different. They were imposed on their world, on their landscape, on their former fields and commons and sometimes even on their former homes. It seems likely that parks represented three interlinked aspects of their lives: powerlessness, lowliness of rank, and

separation or exclusion. Peasant economies must have been seriously compromised by the creation of parks, but presumably with little or no discussion. Many farming hamlets were removed and lines of park boundaries appear to show no flexibility towards the peasant. They cut across open fields and commons, and caused established roads to be re-routed. In addition to all this, the tenant was also often obliged to pay labour services in the park, attending at chases, or repairing pales. Although peasants already knew their rank well enough, the deer park acted as a vivid reminder of their place in the social structure.

Conclusions

Designed not only to keep deer in, but also to keep people out, the park also showed the peasant that they were separate and excluded. This was especially meaningful when the park enclosed land that had been previously open and accessible to the peasants, and indeed had been worked by them. This separation of the elements of society was mirrored elsewhere in the later medieval world. Castles and great houses were becoming more compartmentalised, with the lord and guests increasingly separated from the rest of the household (exemplified in Cornwall by the accommodation provision at Restormel Castle, the country house or hunting lodge set within Cornwall's greatest park). Priests in their chancels were also being increasingly screened off from their congregations in the nave and aisles.

Increasingly sophisticated later medieval burial practices intended to guide the newly dead through purgatory also reinforced the developing awareness of the importance of the individual, as opposed to the communal. The deer park, enclosing and appropriating a significant part of previously open and accessible countryside, was part of this increasing fragmentation of the inherited world. It is usually the earliest example of restricted outdoor space, of explicitly private property. Running newly diverted roads round their perimeters was effective landscape design: travellers had in the tall pale to their side a close view of the reason for their detour, the property of a powerful person. Deer parks, landscape-scale signals of changing ways of perceiving and doing things, in this case the laying of the foundations of our own individualised society, might have helped such an ideology trickle down the social scale. It is in the thirteenth century, not long after the earliest Cornish parks were created, that we get the earliest clear examples of social separation at the peasant level of Cornish society: the creation of private inner rooms in longhouses, and the enclosure of open field systems and the farming of individual holdings.

Medieval deer parks were, then, designed landscapes in which there was participation, movement, and occasional noise. They were designed landscapes that were experienced as much as contemplated. This active element may be the main difference between medieval deer parks and the more serene landscape parks of the early modern period, more peacefully and passively observed from particular viewpoints. The earlier parks are also similar to the eighteenth and nineteenth century ones in that they were more than just status symbols. They were dynamic creations, reflecting changes in society and helping to stimulate further change.

Reference

Herring, P, (2003) *Cornish medieval deer parks*. In: Wilson-North, R (Ed.) *The Lie of the Land, Aspects of the archaeology and history of the designed landscape in the South West of England*. The Mint Press, Exeter

Deer Parks in South Yorkshire: the documentary and landscape evidence

Melvyn Jones
Sheffield Hallam University

Introduction

Medieval deer parks were symbols of status and wealth. In South Yorkshire, they were created by the nobility and were also attached to monasteries. There were also two royal deer parks: Conisbrough Park, formerly the property of the de Warenne family that reverted to the Crown in the fourteenth century and Kimberworth Park that became crown property for a period in the late fifteenth century. As all deer were deemed to belong to the Crown, from the beginning of the thirteenth century landowners were supposed to obtain a licence from the king to create a park, although this appears not to have been necessary if the proposed park was not near a royal forest. The medieval parks at Conisbrough and Sheffield - now disappeared from the landscape except for place-names and some stretches of the boundary bank in the case of Conisbrough, and two important buildings (see below) in the case of Sheffield - predated the issuing of royal licences and so must have been of twelfth century or even earlier, possibly Saxon, origin. Thomas de Furnival, lord of the manor of Sheffield, when asked to explain before the *Quo Warranto* enquiry of 1281 by what right he held Sheffield deer park, said his family had held it (like the right to hold a market) since the Norman Conquest of 1066.

More commonly issued by the crown was the right of free warren that gave a landowner the right to hunt certain animals - pheasant, partridge, hare, rabbit, badger, polecat, and pine marten - within a prescribed area. This was often the forerunner to the fencing of demesne land to create a deer park. Searches of parish histories, principally Hunter's two-volume *South Yorkshire* (Hunter, 1828-31) reveals that more than eighty grants of free warren were given in the medieval period in South Yorkshire

and that in nearly a third of the cases, a deer park is known to have been subsequently created (Jones, 1996).

Most of the deer parks in South Yorkshire were created by the heads of the great Norman dynasties whose ancestors had accompanied the Conqueror to England in 1066. These included the de Warennes of Conisbrough Castle, who had parks at Conisbrough and Hatfield, the de Furnivals, who had a park at Sheffield and were also granted a licence to create a park at Whiston in 1316, and the de Buslis of Tickhill Castle who had a park at Tinsley. They were also created by other local lords of Norman origin such as the Fitzwilliams, Bosvilles, Chaworths and de Vavasors.

Religious houses were also granted permission to create parks in South Yorkshire. Some abbots and priors hunted in their parks - one of the secular practices of which they were accused by Henry VIII. A contemporary record states that Richard de Wombwell, prior of Nostell Priory from 1372-85, was fond of hunting. Significantly, the priory was granted free warren on its lands at Swinton, Thurnscoe and Great Houghton (where there is still a wood called Little Park) during his term of office. Besides Nostell Priory, other religious houses from outside the region were granted free warren on their South Yorkshire properties, for example Rufford Abbey and Worksop Priory, both in Nottinghamshire, and Bolton Abbey in Craven. One of the properties of Bolton Abbey on which they had a grant of free warren was at Wentworth Woodhouse, an antecedent of the surviving Wentworth Park (the only remaining deer park in South Yorkshire). Monk Bretton Priory was granted free warren on its lands at Rainborough in Brampton Bierlow township and there is still a large wood there called Rainborough Park.

The South Yorkshire Deer Parks

At least twenty-seven deer parks were created in medieval South Yorkshire. Nationally the great age of park creation was the century and a half between 1200 and 1350, a period of growing population and agricultural prosperity. Landowners had surplus wealth and there were still sufficient areas of waste on which to create parks. In South Yorkshire, the majority of grants of free warren, which as already noted were often the forerunners of the creation of deer parks, were given in the period from 1250 to 1325 when forty-four grants were made. Significantly, no grants of free warren were given for thirty years following the Black Death (1349), but then there were twenty-one grants between 1379 and 1400. The last known medieval royal licence to create a deer park was given in 1491-92 when Brian Sandford was granted permission to create a park at Thorpe Salvin. This grant is also notable for the fact that it was accompanied by a gift of twelve does from the king's park at Conisbrough '*towards the storing of his parc at Thorp*' (Hunter, 1828, p. 309). The last-known local licence was granted to the second Viscount Castleton in 1637 by King Charles I, to create a deer park at Sandbeck. The licence states that Viscount Castleton was given permission to make separate with pales, walls, or hedges 500 acres or thereabouts of land, meadow, pasture, gorse, heath, wood, underwood, woodland tenements, and hereditaments to make a park where deer and other wild animals might be grazed and kept (Rodgers, 1998).

Deer parks were still being created or re-stocked in South Yorkshire in the eighteenth century. John Spencer, of Cannon Hall, for example, remodelled his parkland in the 1760s, building a new boundary wall and a ha-ha to separate the park from the gardens. Once these works were completed he set about re-stocking his park with fallow deer. He recorded in his diary on Wednesday 3 February 1762 that '*The Gamekeeper returned from Sprodborough with*

twenty bucks'. Two days later he noted that '*deer from Sir George Armytage's of Kirk Lees Hall*' had been brought to his park and the next day he recorded that he had been to Gunthwaite and '*took the deer out of Gunthwaite Park & put them into my park*'. By the end of the week, he had a herd of eighty-nine deer in his park at Cannon Hall (Spencer Stanhope Muniments, 60633).

The creation of a park, emparkment, involved enclosing an area of land with a fence to keep the deer and other game inside and predators (in the early days wolves) and poachers outside. The fence - the park pale - consisted either of cleft oak vertical pales with horizontal railings, often set on a bank, or a stone wall. As parks could vary in size from under 100 acres to several thousand acres (Sheffield Park at its greatest extent covered nearly 2,500 acres and was eight miles in circumference) fencing was a major initial and recurring expense. Because of this, the most economical shape for a deer park was a circle or a rectangle with rounded corners, as was the case throughout South Yorkshire.

Deer parks were not created primarily for hunting although hunting did take place in the larger parks. The deer were carefully farmed (Birrell, 1992). Besides their status symbol role their main function was to provide for their owners a reliable source of food for the table, supplies of wood and timber, and in some cases quarried stone, coal and ironstone. They were, therefore, an integral part of the local economy. The killing of deer for venison was often reserved for special occasions. A good local example was the funeral of the fifth Earl of Shrewsbury in 1560 when, for the great dinner held in Sheffield Castle following the funeral, fifty does (female fallow deer) and twenty-nine red deer were killed and cooked (Drury, 1897).

The deer in most parks were fallow deer, which were not native to Britain and were probably introduced by the Normans. Fallow deer were much easier to contain within a park than the native red and roe deer. Locally both fallow and red deer were kept in parks. In John Harrison's Survey of the Manor of Sheffield in

1637, the park there was said to be '*not meanly furnished with fallow Deare, the number of them at present is one Thousand*' (Ronksley, 1908, p. 3). Nearly a century later, when Daniel Defoe rode through Tankersley Park he commented that he had seen '*...the largest red deer that, I believe, are in this part of Europe. One of the hinds, I think, was larger than my horse...*' (Defoe 1727, Vol. 3, p.59). Besides deer, hares, rabbits (also introduced by the Normans and kept in burrows in artificially made mounds) and game birds were kept in the medieval parks of South Yorkshire. Herds of cattle, flocks of sheep and pigs were also grazed there. Another important feature of South Yorkshire's medieval deer parks were fishponds to provide an alternative to meat in Lent and on fast days.

Although there are records of parks without trees, deer parks usually consisted of woodland and areas largely cleared of trees. The park livestock could graze in the open areas and find cover in the wooded areas. The cleared areas, called launds or plains, consisted of grassland or heath with scattered trees. The king's park keeper at Conisbrough Park in the second half of the fifteenth century was referred to in a document written in French as '*Laundier et Palisser de n're park de Connesburgh*'(Hunter, 1828, p. 114). Many of the trees in the launds would have been pollarded, i.e., trees cut at least six feet from the ground leaving a massive lower trunk called a bolling above which a continuous crop of new growth sprouted out of reach of the grazing deer, sheep and cattle. In the launds regeneration of trees was restricted because of continual grazing and new trees were only able to grow in the protection of thickets of hawthorn and holly. Some of the unpollarded trees might reach a great age and size and were much sought after for major building projects. Some enormous trees were recorded in Sheffield Park in the seventeenth century (see below).

The woods within deer parks were managed in different ways. Some woods were 'holted', i.e. they consisted of single-stemmed trees grown for their timber like a modern plantation. Most woods were coppiced and were surrounded by a bank or wall to keep out the grazing animals during the early years of re-growth. Later in the coppice cycle, the deer would have been allowed into the coppice woods. There were also in South Yorkshire's deer parks, separate woods, or special compartments within coppice woods in which the dominant tree was holly and which were called holly hags. The holly was cut in winter for the deer and other park livestock.

Between the late fifteenth and eighteenth centuries, many medieval deer parks either changed their function and hence their appearance, or, more commonly, disappeared altogether. When a landlord was absent (his main country seat may have been in another parish or county) or where his hall lay some distance away from his medieval park, there was increased possibility that the park may disappear altogether. John Speed's map of the West Riding of Yorkshire published in 1610 shows only ten surviving deer parks in South Yorkshire: at Wortley, Tankersley, Brierley, Sheffield, Kimberworth, Thrybergh, Conisbrough, Treeton, Aston, and Austerfield (see Figure 1). Only the outline of Tankersley Park has survived to the present day in any recognisable form.

Well-wooded parks often simply became large coppice woods. Examples of the reversion to managed woodland in South Yorkshire are Cowley Park, Hesley Park, Shirecliffe Park, and Tinsley Park. Cowley Park and Hesley Park, for example, became coppice woods of 163 and 135 acres respectively. A large part of the former Shirecliffe Park, survived into the twentieth century in the form of a large wood called Shirecliffe Old Park, which in Harrision's 1637 survey of the manor of Sheffield was described as 'A Spring wood called Shirtcliffe parke' and covered 143 acres (Ronksley, 1908, p. 228). Tinsley Park by 1657 was a compartmented wood that was let by its owner, the second Earl of Strafford to the ironmaster, Lionel Copley, for felling for charcoal making. It covered 413 acres and comprised ten coppice woods and three holts (Wentworth Woodhouse Muniments, D778). Rainborough Park at Brampton became a coppice wood and the

Figure 1: Part of John Speed's map of the West Riding of Yorkshire, 1610, showing ten surviving medieval deer parks in South Yorkshire: A - Wortley; B - Tankersley; C - Brierley; D - Sheffield; E - Kimberworth; F - Thrybergh; G - Conisbrough; H - Treeton; I - Aston; J - Austerfield. The four unidentified parks in the eastern part of the map were in Nottinghamshire.

shape of the modern wood, a long rectangle with rounded corners, still suggests that it was once a fenced enclosure for deer.

Other medieval parks simply reverted wholly or largely to farmland. South Yorkshire examples include Aston Park, Brierley Old Park, and Conisbrough Park. The outline of a

small park at Aston, still survives in the agricultural landscape as a rectangle with rounded corners (see Figure 2). This small park appears to be the one shown on John Speed's map of 1610 and seems to be the one created by Osbert de Arches who had been granted a right of free warren in 1256-57. The park became part of a farm called Old Park Farm.

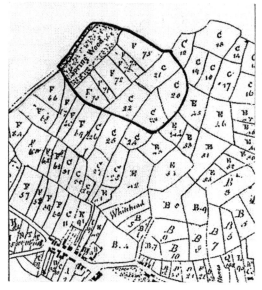

Figure 2: The outline of Aston Park, shown by the bold line, of typically rounded rectangle shape, and with the parish boundary on the north side. Source: Release and settlement of Aston pursuant to a marriage settlement, 15th September, 1775. 301-F, Rotherham MBC, Archives and Local Studies.

Brierley Old Park, north-east of Barnsley, was created by Geffrey Neville following the grant of a right of free warren in 1279-80. It is not known when disparkment took place but this probably occurred in the seventeenth century. Like Aston Park, it appears on John Speed's map of 1610. It is now mostly farmland but most of the long eastern and western sides of its perimeter still survive as ghost features in the form of curving field boundaries on large-scale Ordnance Survey maps (Figure 3). Lying in the middle of the southern half of the park are the remains of a moated site called the Hall Steads. In the northern part of the park is a manor house that was substantially repaired in 1632. Hunter, writing in 1831, suggested that the Hall Steads '*might have been for defence and security, and the manour for refreshment and pleasure, like the castle and "manour" in Sheffield*.' (Hunter, 1831, p. 407).

Conisbrough Park was a large park attached to the castle at Conisbrough, the former royal estate at Conisbrough having been granted by King William to William de Warenne after the Norman Conquest in 1066. As noted earlier, the park appears to have been in existence from at least the twelfth century. In the fourteenth

century it became crown property once again as did the former de Warenne deer park and chase at Hatfield. Today it is difficult to delineate exactly the boundaries of Conisbrough Park. Its general location and extent can be identified from surviving park-related place names that dot the farming landscape that now occupies the area once covered by the park, and there is a general area to the south of Conisbrough called Conisbrough Parks. This also contains Park Lane, Conisbrough Parks Cottages, Conisbrough Parks Farm, and Conisbrough Lodge. Weak boundary banks have also survived beside Park Lane towards Firsby.

While hundreds of medieval deer parks were disappearing, many others took on a new lease of life and many new parks were created. This was because the concept of the park was changing. Its primary function changed from being a game preserve and a valuable source of wood and timber to being the adornment of a country house. New residences were built within existing parks and the park boundaries extended. The parks surrounding the new country houses that sprang up in the sixteenth and seventeen centuries, were still essentially deer parks, although grazing cattle were a much

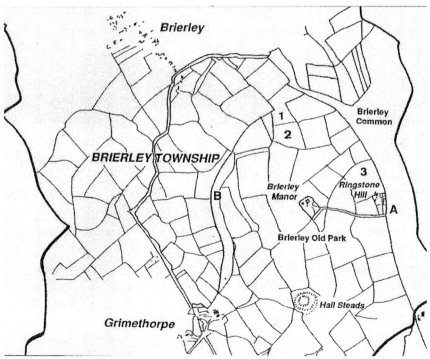

Figure 3: Selective trace from the OS 25-inch sheet published in 1894 showing the curving boundaries (A and B) of the former deer park at Brierley. The numbered fields are Park Gate Close (1), Park Gate (2) and Park Close (3).

more common sight than in the medieval period, with both the deer and the cattle being an aesthetic backdrop to the house as much as a source of food. Wentworth Woodhouse, the eighteenth century residence of the Marquises of Rockingham and in the nineteenth and twentieth centuries of their successors, the Earls Fitzwilliam, provides the clearest South Yorkshire example of this change (Jones, 1995). In 1732 Thomas Wentworth (later the first Marquis) embarked on the building of his magnificent Palladian mansion and the improvement of the surrounding park, or as he put it in a letter to his son, to '*beautifye the country and do the work ordered by God himself*'. He extended the park until it was more than nine miles in circumference, created '*a Serpentine river*' and built a number of monuments, including a Doric temple and an Ionic temple. The sixth Earl Fitzwilliam in the second half of the nineteenth century also added a herd of bison to the red and fallow deer that grazed in the park.

Detailed case studies

Below are detailed case studies of three South Yorkshire deer parks that illustrate many of the general points made above. The first case study is of Kimberworth Park, the history of which is charted from its creation in the early thirteenth century to its eventual disparkment in the mid-seventeenth century. Documentary and landscape evidence are used to identify the park boundaries. The second case study, of Sheffield deer park, provides details of the management of the park in the medieval and early modern period, and then of its gradual disparkment, particularly after the lords of the manor left Sheffield for residence elsewhere. The third case study is of Tankersley Park with particular emphasis on an analysis of an early eighteenth century engraving of the park. This shows its layout in minute detail and on the details of its gradual disappearance in the late eighteenth and nineteenth centuries as a result of ironstone mining.

Kimberworth Park

The first documentary record of a park at Kimberworth is in the Feet of Fines (agreements over disputes about land ownership) for 7th December 1226 (*Yorkshire Archaeological Society, Record Series*, **Vol. LXII**). The document records that the Abbot of Kirkstead Abbey in Lincolnshire and Robert de Vipont, lord of the manor of Kimberworth, were in dispute over access to common land in the manor for the abbot's cattle. Under an agreement of 1161 with the then lord of the manor, Richard de Busli, the monks of Kirkstead Abbey had been given access to the common land to mine ironstone and erect two furnaces and two forges for smelting and forging the iron and in order to collect dead wood for their furnaces and forges. By 1226, the abbot claimed that the lord of the manor had set up a dyke (i.e., a wall or embankment) barring access to part of the common. The proceedings make it clear that the dyke was a park wall or bank of the 'park of Kimberworth' and the abbot's rights of access were annulled.

The next known record of Kimberworth Park is in the Hundred Rolls of 1276. The Hundred Rolls were records of enquiries made on behalf of King Edward I about the privileges claimed by the nobility, clergy and others that diverted profits from the royal coffers into private hands. In 1276, the lord of the manor, Robert de Vipont (who had died in 1265) and his heirs, were accused of exceeding the bounds of the free warren in Kimberworth and of including within the deer park a portion of the king's highway (Hunter, 1831, p. 27). In the *Quo Warranto* proceedings of 1292, Idonea de Leybourn, Robert de Vipont's daughter, was asked by what right she claimed the privilege of having a deer park. Secondly, she was charged with constructing a deer leap (*saltatorium*) to entice deer into her park, which was to the disadvantage of the king because deer from the king's forest were likely to become part of the Kimberworth Park herd. The jury was satisfied that she had not created a park unlawfully but had inherited it from her father. On the matter of the deer leap, the jury was satisfied that it was not to the detriment of the king because the nearest royal forest (Sherwood) was fifteen leagues away, and the chases of the de Warenne family (Hatfield Chase to the east of Doncaster) and of the de Furnivals (Rivelin Chase to the west of Sheffield) were in between (Guest, 1879, pp. 583-84).

By the late fifteenth century, the manor and park were the property of the crown and in 1487 in the hands of a newly appointed bailiff and park keeper. The office of park keeper included herbage and pannage (Hunter, 1831, p. 28). What this probably means is that the park keeper was able to augment his income by letting grazing in the park. Just over a century later (c.1600), by which time the park was the property of the Earls of Shrewsbury (who resided in Sheffield Castle), there was a coal pit in the park (Meredith, 1965). At about the same date it was recorded that there were 300 acres of coppice wood in the park '*all redie to be coled*' (Shrewsbury Papers in Lambeth Palace Library, Ms 698, Fol. 3). The park still contained fallow deer in 1635 (Hunter, 1831, p. 303), but by 1649 momentous changes were beginning to take place. In a rental of 1649 part of the park had become a farm, called Park Gate Farm, later records showing that it covered 141 acres. By 1671, the whole of the park had been leased; the farm as in 1649, and the rest of the park, amounting to 605 acres, had been leased to Lionel Copley, an ironmaster. His main interests were the coal and ironstone reserves that lay beneath the park and the surviving coppice woods that could be felled and made into charcoal (Arundel Castle Manuscripts, ACM S131). By the time of a survey of 1732, by which time, the former park area was the property of the Earl of Effingham, complete disparkment had taken place and, apart from the surviving woodlands, was laid out as farms.

The extent of the park can be mapped with a high degree of confidence based on a 'General Survey of Kimberworth Park' carried out in 1802 (Fairbank Collection, Rot 45R and Rot 46L) and an estate map drawn by R Consterdine in 1834. The main features of these surveys are summarised in Figure 4. This shows that the park had formerly extended for nearly two miles in a south-easterly direction from Park Gate Farm to Bradgate. The northern boundary of the park coincided with the township boundary between Kimberworth and Greasbrough and part of the western boundary with the parish boundary between Kimberworth and Ecclesfield parish. The total acreage of the former park in the 1802 survey was just under 618 acres. If Gallery Bottom Wood (not included in the survey) and Scholes Coppice (which had been sold) are added, the total comes to 749 acres - just three acres more than the acreage of the park that had been leased in 1671. Field names clearly pointing at the former existence of a deer park were Gallery Bottom Plain, three closes including the name 'park' and five including the name 'warren'. Map and landscape evidence show that Scholes Coppice was almost certainly once part of the park. The southern part of the lane to the west of Scholes Coppice now known as Scholes Lane was called Park Lane in a deed of 1699 and it will be noted that it takes a violent swing to the south-west as if it has met a barrier, possibly the park boundary. Further, the boundary of Scholes Coppice in the north-west is in the form of a bank surmounted with a wall and with an internal ditch. There is one other set of intriguing landscape features within the boundaries of the former park. In a narrow valley at the southern extremity of Gallery Bottom are the silted remains of three ponds. Stone-built sluices are still in place in the dam walls (earthern banks). The bottom pond is 30 metres long, the middle pond is 38 metres long and the top pond, which is more difficult to define, is more than 60 metres long. To the south of the line of ponds are the remains of a stone wall. The ponds may be the park fishponds and the old stone wall the remains of the park wall.

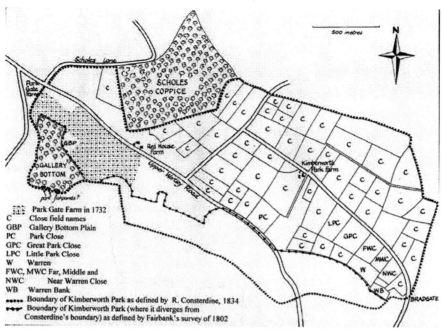

Figure 4: Kimberworth Park as defined by Fairbank's survey of 1802 and by R. Consterdine in 1834.

Sheffield Park

This deer park, which at its greatest extent covered 2,462 acres (nearly 1,000 hectares) and was eight miles (13 kilometres) in circumference, came right up to the eastern edge of the town of Sheffield (Figure 5). It had a typical shape, a rounded rectangle which was the most economic shape for fencing. The park pale appears to have been, in the late medieval period at least, a high cleft-oak paling fence. We know this from a surviving manorial account roll of 1441-42, which states that a payment was paid to John Legge and John Gotsone for repairing defects in the rails and paling around the park (Thomas, 1924). The park pale had three functions: to keep the deer in and to keep predators and poachers out. The temptation was often too much for certain sections of the population and at the court leet of the manor of Sheffield in 1578 six local men were each fined five shillings '*for huntinge the hare within my Lordes Parke ... to the disturbance of my Lordes game there, & killed one deare & dyd hyte an other deare*'(Wigfull, 1929).

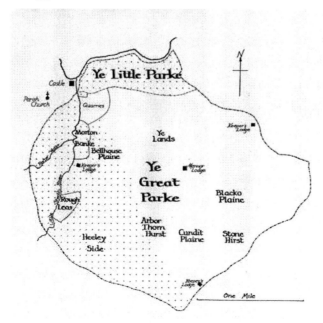

Figure 5: Sheffield Park in 1637 after Harrison (1637) and Scurfield (1986). The stippled areas are those parts of the park let to tenants.

The function of a deer park changed over time. The manorial roll for 1441-42, for example, gives a detailed glimpse into the functioning of Sheffield deer park in the mid-fifteenth century. By this time, substantial parts of the park were let to tenants. There were leased grazing pastures and hay meadows and a '*mine of sea-coal*'. Income was also derived from allowing holly trees to be cropped (for fodder), from the pannage of pigs, from the sale of timber of felled trees, and from the sale of a parcel of underwood. There was also charcoal made from the branches of trees where they were being cleared to make a new pasture, and from the sale of cinders (from burnt coal?) to the dyers of Chesterfield. The park also supplied firewood for the castle, timber for building repairs at the castle stables, brushwood, and stakes to repair the dam and weir of the fulling mill, and quarries in the park supplied both wall stone and stone slates for house building and repairs to the manorial corn mill and fulling mill.

By the seventeenth century, the park was in decline but still contained a number of very important features. By 1637, when John Harrison carried out his survey of the manor of Sheffield more than 971 acres (more than a third of the park) had been let to tenants. This included the whole of the northern part of the park, called the Little Park, all that part of the Great Park to the west of the Sheaf, and all but two enclosures amounting to 80 acres in the western third of the Great Park to the east of the Sheaf (see Figure 5). The tenanted parts of the park in 1637 were a mixture of arable, grazing, and meadowland, and also included a coppice wood on Morton Bank. They also included Heeley Side which was grazing land in which there were coal pits which Harrison said '*yieldeth great profit unto the Lord*' (Ronksley, 1908, p.51).

Those parts of the park still managed as a deer park in 1637, contained 1,000 fallow deer, including 200 antlered bucks, or as Harrison put it '*Deare of Auntler*'. Harrison named the various parts of the park including some with woodland names including Arbor Thorn Hirst and Stone Hirst (hyrst = a wooded hill) but they

would only have been covered with scrub woods of hawthorn and holly. Other names mentioned by Harrison such as ye Lands, Cundit Plaine, Blacko Plaine and Bellhouse Plaine suggest grazing areas with scattered trees. Ye Lands is probably a corruption of laund. The launds and plains would certainly have contained a scattering of trees, some of them pollarded above the height of grazing animals, and many unpollarded oaks of a great size and age. Some of the oak trees in the park were described in great detail by John Evelyn in his book *Silva*, first published in 1670. He appears to have obtained his information from Edmund Morphy, one of the Duke of Norfolk's woodwards. Evelyn said that in 1646 there were 100 trees whose combined value was £1000. He described one oak tree in the park whose trunk was thirteen feet in diameter and another which was ten yards in circumference. On Conduit Plain (the Cundit Plaine of Harrison's 1637 survey), Evelyn reported that there was one oak tree whose boughs were so far spreading that he estimated (giving all his calculations) that 251 horses could stand in its shade. He also described another massive oak that when cut down yielded 1,400 '*wairs*' which were planks two yards long and one yard wide and 20 cords from its branches. Finally, he described another oak, that when felled and lying on its side was so massive that two men on horseback on either side of it could not see each other's hat crowns (Evelyn, 1706 edition, pp. 229-230).

There were two important buildings standing in the park by the beginning of the sixteenth century. In the north-western corner, beside the ponds which eventually formed the water power for a second manorial corn mill, stood the Hall in the Ponds. Dendrochronological analysis shows that this timber-framed building, which survives in part today as the *Old Queen's Head* public house, was built of timber felled between 1503-1510 (Univ. of Nottingham, Tree Dating Laboratory, January 1992). The building is jettied on the south, west and east sides, has close-studded walls, a king post roof, and carved heads on the exterior of the ground-floor posts. The two-storeyed building originally had a single two-bayed room on each floor, with the first floor room open to the roof. In an inventory of its contents compiled in 1582, the building was said to contain '*peces of paynted hangings*' and window and chimney pieces of canvas, a trestle table, two '*buffet formes*', a '*buffet stoule*', a still, a flagon, pewter dishes and a spit. These all suggest it was used for the preparation of meals and dining in a very comfortable setting. It may originally have been a banqueting house for the lord of the manor and his guests at the end of a day's hunting, fishing, and fowling in the park. Significantly, in a letter from an estate official in Sheffield to the seventh Earl of Shrewsbury and his Countess in 1599 (who were in London) an account is given of stocking with fish 'the Pond mill dam' for the Earl's use (Meredith, 1965).

On a much larger scale than the Hall in the Ponds, was the Manor Lodge, located near the centre of the park with glorious views in all directions. This was originally a hunting lodge, converted into a comfortable country residence by George, the 4th Earl of Shrewsbury. Harrison in his survey of 1637 described it as '*being fairely built with stone & Timber with an Inward & an outward Court 2 Gardens & 3 Yards*' (Ronksley, 1908, p.48). Mostly in ruins now, only the Turret House near the entrance to the site still survives largely intact. On the second floor of the Turret House is a room with an original Elizabethan fireplace and decorated plaster ceiling. The Manor Lodge is famous because Mary, Queen of Scots, spent much time here during her long imprisonment under George, 6th Earl of Shrewsbury.

After the death of the seventh Earl of Shrewsbury in 1616, the lords of the manor never resided in Sheffield again, the park was reduced in size, and eventually let to tenants, both agricultural and industrial. The manor lodge was also occupied in part by a tenant and then was largely dismantled in the early eighteenth century. In the late eighteenth century, the town of Sheffield began its inevitable long-term expansion across the park, at first in the form of a planned extension of streets on a gridiron plan, each street having a name associated with the absent lords of the manor. Then in the nineteenth century, tightly packed back-to-back housing and small workshops covered Park Hill, that part of the former park nearest the town. These were demolished in the 1950s and 1960s and replaced by high-rise blocks. Most significantly, between 1921 and 1939, the Manor estate, containing 3,600 houses, was laid out on Garden City principles across a large expanse of the former park. Now the only green space left is Norfolk Park, a 70-acre municipal park opened in 1848.

Tankersley Park

Virtually nothing is known of the medieval history of this 750-acre park (Hey, 1975). A right of free warren was granted to the lord of the manor, Hugh de Elland, in 1303-04 and that, presumably, subsequently the park was created. Only one reference to the park is known between the fourteenth and early seventeenth centuries when Henry Savile in a law suit of 1527 was said to have been 'hunting at dere wythe houndes in hys parke at Tankersley' (*Yorkshire Archaeological Society, Record Series*, **Vol. LXX** (1926), 49). The Saviles had inherited the estate from the Ellands in the late fourteenth century, and in the sixteenth century, they built a hall in the centre of the park.

Thomas Wentworth, the first Earl of Strafford, purchased the Tankersley estate with the park sometime between 1614-1635. The Wentworths and their successors, the Watson-Wentworths and the Wentworth-Fitzwilliams, resided just a few miles to the east of Tankersley at Wentworth Woodhouse. In the eighteenth century, they built their magnificent Palladian mansion (they began building in 1732) at Wentworth Woodhouse and surrounded it with a large landscaped park. From that time, Tankersley Park went into decline, at first shrunken through enclosure for farming and then mined for ironstone from shallow bell pits and gin pits and through deep shaft mining. An early eighteenth century engraving of the park made for the first Marquis of Rockingham has survived which shows many interesting features of its layout and management for deer. Unusually there is also a very full record of ironstone mining in the park from the late eighteenth century until the 1870s, during which time that part of the park still functioning as a deer park was steadily decreased in size, until the late 1850s. The remaining deer were then removed to Wentworth Woodhouse.

The engraving (Figure 6 (a)) dates from the late 1720s. According to the titling below the engraving, when it was done, the owner, Thomas Wentworth, who had inherited the estate from his father in 1723, was Knight of the Bath. In 1728, he was created Baron Wentworth of Malton and in 1734 Baron of Harrowden, Viscount Higham of Higham Ferrers and Baron of Wath and Earl of Malton. He became Baron Rockingham in 1745 and Marquis of Rockingham in 1746. The engraving shows the park, in the form of a bird's- eye view looking from the east. Figure 6 (b) shows the information in the engraving in map form, based on the first edition O.S. six-inch sheet, with a number of key features identified. One odd feature of the engraving is that the orientation of Tankersley parish church, which lies just outside the northern boundary of the deer park, has been changed from west-to-east to south-to-north so that the observer gets a full view of the tower, porch, nave, and chancel.

The park is a typical shape, rectangular with rounded corners in the south-west and south-east. Being in 'stone wall country', it is completely surrounded by a wall of locally-quarried Coal Measures sandstone rather than by a bank and cleft-oak pales and railings. In the centre of the park is the residence built by the once owner of the park, Thomas Savile, dating from the Elizabethan period, and known as Tankersley Old Hall from the eighteenth century and earlier as the Lodge. The hall seems to have been the successor to the moated manor house that lay outside the park to the north of the parish church, the moated site, by the early eighteenth century, being occupied by the rectory. The gardens and pleasure grounds of the hall are surrounded by a pale fence. Along Harley Dike, the stream running through

the park and escaping through the park wall on the engraving, are four fishponds, the largest one called the Lawn Pond on late eighteenth century maps. The group of buildings to the south of the Lawn Pond are probably the park keeper's. In a local surveyor's field-book connected with a survey of the manor of Tankersley in 1772, they are described as lying around a farmyard and occupied by the second Marquis of Rockingham (the successor of Thomas Wentworth for whom the engraving was made).

The park is compartmented with the two largest compartments (which both contain deer on the engraving), separated by an area of dense woodland. One of these is the area in the south of the park shown on later maps as the Burfitts and the other area containing the deer shed named on some maps as '*the Lawn*'. Two other distinct and walled areas were the Warren in the south-west and the Paddocks in the north. There was also a small wood shown on the engraving on the north-western margin of the park. On nineteenth century maps, this is called the Folly Spring, a 'spring wood' in South Yorkshire being almost invariably a coppice-with-standards. The eastern part of the park was divided into a series of walled enclosures, one of which is shown to hold deer, but others that do not and which may at that time have been tenanted. In a lease of the park and the Lodge to Sir Richard Fanshawe in 1653, three-quarters of a century before the engraving was completed, it was stated that certain parts of the park including the Paddocks and Swift Bank had been '*divided and severed from the deere*' and were or had recently been in the occupation of tenants (Hall, 1937).

A feature of the park, strongly emphasised in the engraving, was that it was dotted with magnificent veteran trees, including oaks and yews. Hunter (1831, p. 303) quotes one traveller who said that the '*Talbot yew*' in the park was so large that '*a man on horseback might turn round in it*'. The first edition six-inch Ordnance Survey map (Sheet 282, published in 1853) even points out the oak tree in the park '*in which it is said Lord Strafford was arrested*'. However, the first Earl of Strafford was in fact

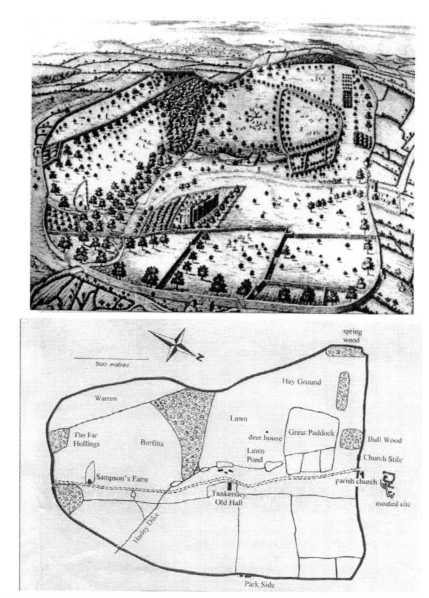

Figures 6 (a) and 6 (b): Figure 6 (a) shows the engraving of Tankersley Park dating from the 1720s. Figure 6 (b) shows the information on the engraving in map form with a number of features and areas identified by name.

arrested for treason in London and executed in 1640. Late nineteenth century photographs have also survived showing magnificent pollarded horse chestnuts in the park.

The park also shows the careful way in which provision was made for the deer, which at Tankersley were mostly red deer. There were, besides the hundreds of acres of grass sward in which they could graze and the woodlands in which they could take cover, a number of special provisions made for the animals. There was the special area, the Warren, where hinds could be kept and looked after during the breeding season, and three specific ways in which extra feed in winter could be provided. First, between the Paddocks and Folly Spring, was an area called the Hay Ground where the

grass was cut for hay for the deer. The 1653 lease specified that two loads of hay should be provided in winter for every hundred deer (the lease specifies that the number of deer should be increased to 280). The hay was stored in the deer house, deer shed or rotunda that is shown clearly on the engraving. Mangers would be erected at the deer house in which the hay was placed and replenished. In addition to hay, the 1653 lease specified that the deer had also to be fed in winter '*with holley to be cutt therein*'. This was often grown in special woods or compartments in woods called in South Yorkshire 'holly hags'. The engraving shows a walled wooded enclosure in the south-eastern corner of the park. On late eighteenth century maps this is called the Far Hollings. Bull Wood that is also shown on the engraving, survives to this day, and is full of holly and may have been another holly hag in the park.

The engraving also shows the first stage in the disparkment of Tankersley Park in the form of buildings in their small enclosure not far inside the southern boundary of the park. This was Sampson's Farm that appears to have been carved out of the park in the late 1720s and early 1730s. A stone on one of the surviving cottages bears the date 1729. In March 1732 *eleven thousand quicksetts* were planted as new field boundaries and in the autumn of 1732 it is recorded that a barn was being built on the farm using stone from Tankersley Old Hall which was evidently being dismantled (Clayton, 1962). As the century proceeded, more and more of the park was converted to tenanted farmland. By 1772 when a detailed survey of Tankersley was carried out (Fairbank Collection, A288) more than two-thirds of the area of the park (nearly 500 acres) was in the hands of nine tenants and only 265 acres remained in the hands of the second Marquis. Despite the reduction in the size of the park the second Marquis and Countess must have retained a great deal of affection for Tankersley Park, as in the 1760s the Marquis built a stone summer house / observatory called 'Lady's Folly' at the highest point in the park on the hay ground with extensive views in every direction.

However, change that is even more dramatic was to follow, for the park is underlain by seams of coal measure ironstone - the Tankersley Ironstone, Swallow Wood Ironstone and Lidgett Ironstone - and these ironstones were systematically exploited between 1795 and 1879 to supply the Elescar and Milton ironworks in Hoyland township to the east (Jones, 1988 and Jones, 1995). The first large-scale and long-term exploitation of the Tankersley Ironstone that lay beneath the park began in 1795 by John Darwin & Co who had leased the new Elsecar Ironworks. The furnace was run directly by Earl Fitzwilliam from 1827. These early workings were in the southern part of the park and lasted until 1831. The mining was undertaken by sinking shallow bell pits and gin-pits (a superior type of bell pit with

ironstone raised and the men and boys lowered and raised by a horse gin as opposed to a windlass). They were not working in an untried area, an estate map of 1849 showing old and new pits inside the southern part of the park. The mined area was planted and became Hood Hill Plantation (Jones, 1984). While mining was proceeding in the southern part of the park, exploitation of the Tankersley Ironstone also began to the north of the park boundary in 1801 by the lessees of the Milton Ironworks. These mining operations had extended just into the park itself by 1835. Between 1836 and 1841 the workings were extended southwards. At this point the lessees of the Milton Ironworks were refused permission to sink more shallow pits in the deer park and so, between 1840 and 1850 a deep shaft mine was sunk to exploit a large area of Tankersley Ironstone to west of the Tanksersley Fault. Ironstone mining from shallow pits was resumed in the 1850s and these were never levelled and form the giant 'molehills' on Tankersley Park golf course today. Swallow Wood Ironstone occurs very near the surface in Tankersley Park and was mined from very shallow bell pits between 1823 and c.1852. On cessation of mining, the area was planted as a beech plantation called Bell Ground. Finally, Skiers Spring deep pit was opened in 1849, and until 1879, the remaining Tankersley Ironstone in the park to the east of the Tankersley Fault was mined.

The ironstone mining had the effect, slowly but surely, of leading to total disparkment. Earl Fitzwilliam's mineral agent, Benjamin Biram, noted in his diary on 15th January 1855 that there were 380 fallow deer and 64 red deer at Wentworth and Tankersley (WWM SP 16XV). However, within a year or two the remaining deer at Tankersley were removed to Wentworth. The deer house remained until after 1900, Lady's Folly was dismantled in 1960, and all that remains to remind the visitor that there was a deer park here are the silted up remains of the fishponds and the ruins of Tankersley Old Hall.

References

Primary Sources

The following primary sources are in Sheffield Archives:

Arundel Castle Muniments

Fairbank Collection

Wentworth Woodhouse Muniments

Spencer Stanhope Muniments

Secondary Sources

Birrell, J. (1992) Deer and Deer Farming in Medieval England. *The Agricultural History Review*, **40**, 112-126

Clayton, A. K. (1962) The Break-Up of Tankersley Park. *South Yorkshire Times*, 1 February

Defoe, D. (1727) *A Tour through the Whole Island of Great Britain*. **Vol. 3**, Folio Society edition 1983, London, p. 59

Drury, C. (1897) The Funeral of Francis Talbot, Earl of Shrewsbury at Sheffield, 1560. *Sheffield Miscellany*, Pt 4, p.140

Evelyn, J. (1706 edition) *Silva or a Discourse of Forest Trees*

Hall, T. W. (1937) Tankersley Old Hall and Fanshawe Gate. In: *Incunabula of Sheffield History*,: J.W. Northend Ltd, Sheffield, pp169-202

Hey, D. (1975) The Parks at Tankersley and Wortley. *The Yorkshire Archaeological Journal*, **47**, 109-119.

Hunter, J. (1828-31) *South Yorkshire* (Volume 1, 1828 and Volume 2, 1831) reprinted by E.P. Publishing, Wakefield, 1974

Jones, M. (1988) Combining Estate Records with Census Enumerators. Books to study Nineteenth Century Communities: the case of the Tankersley Ironstone Miners, c. 1850. *Local Population Studies*, **No 41**, 3-27

Jones, M. (1994) Woodland Origins in a South Yorkshire Parish. *The Local Historian*, **16** (2), 73-82

Jones, M. (1995) Rents, Remarks and Observations: The First Marquis of Rockingham's Rent Roll Book. In: Jones. M. (Ed.) *Aspects of Rotherham: Discovering Local History, Volume 1*, Wharncliffe Books, Barnsley, 113-128

Jones, M. (1995) Ironstone Mining at Tankersley in the Nineteenth Century for Elsecar and Milton Ironworks. In: Elliott, B. (Ed.) *Aspects of Barnsley: Discovering Local History, Volume 3*, Wharncliffe Publishing, Barnsley, 89-115

Jones, M. (1996) Deer in South Yorkshire: an Historical Perspective in Jones, M., Rotherham, I.D., &. McCarthy, A. J (Eds.) Deer or the New Woodlands? *The Journal of Practical Ecology and Conservation, Special Publication*, **No 1**, 11-26

Meredith, R. (1965) *Catalogue of the Arundel Castle Manuscripts with a Calendar of the Talbot Letters*. Library and Arts Committee, Sheffield

Rodgers, A. (1998) Deer Parks in the Maltby Area. In: Jones, M. (Ed.) *Aspects of Rotherham: Discovering Local History, Volume 3*, Wharncliffe Publishing, Barnsley, 8-30

Ronksley, J. G. (Ed.) *An exact and perfect Survey of the Manor of Sheffield and other lands by John Harrison, 1637*. Robert White & Co., Worksop

Wigfull, J. R. (1929) The Court Leet of the Manor of Sheffield. *Transactions of the Hunter Archaeological Society*, **III**, 143-154

Yorkshire Archaeological Society (1921) *Feet of Fines for the County of York 1218 to 1231. Record Series*, **Vol. LXII**

Chatsworth: invertebrates and the veteran trees

Roger S. Key

Senior Education Specialist, Natural England
(formerly Senior Invertebrate Specialist)

Introduction

Chatsworth Old Park was notified as a *Site of Special Scientific Interest* (SSSI) in 1998. This was based on the richness of the invertebrate fauna and lichen flora associated with the old oak trees. Using an '*Index of Ecological Continuity*' (Alexander, 1994) the site comes in the top fifty sites for this fauna in the UK. Relatively few sites for saproxylic invertebrates have been notified in areas with such an upland character as Chatsworth, and there are only two other similar sites within that top fifty list. The assumption is that upland (as well as northern) areas may be too cold and damp to support faunas that are as rich as those of southern/lowland sites. Chatsworth's richness almost certainly results from a combination of both the number and the quality of its old trees, the warm aspect of the site (south west facing), and its possible/likely historical contiguity with a once greater expanse of forested landscape, the so-called '*greater Sherwood*' with sites loosely connected with 'Sherwood Forest' sharing a number of highly localised species.

Such indices as described above are largely dependent on the presence of rarities and species with a high fidelity to good quality examples of the habitat, indicator species. Twenty such indicators have been recorded at Chatsworth, but further recording will almost certainly reveal additional such species of interest. While many of the saproxylic species used in evaluating such sites are fairly insignificant in appearance, a few of those from Chatsworth are quite spectacular:

- Net-winged beetle *Pyropterus nigroruber* - scarlet and black - one of the Sherwood specialities

- Tanbark beetle *Callidium violaceum* - large scarlet and metallic blue longhorn in thick oak bark

- Longhorn beetle *Saperda scalaris* - highly patterned large longhorn beetle

- Cobweb beetle *Ctesias serra* - very fuzzy larva covered with tufts of bristles to keep spiders off

Niches of importance for the deadwood beetles at Chatsworth are nearly all associated with the ancient oaks, although one red-listed species, *Ernoporus caucasicus*, is associated with old limes. Of particular importance on old oaks is the existence of various forms of fungal heart decay of the main trunk, resulting in hollows and an accumulation of wood-mould of various consistencies. This is the specific habitat of quite a number of species recorded there. The very thick, rugose bark of oak, usually with some areas that are loose, is also a very important microhabitat.

A particular surprise at Chatsworth is the relative paucity of nectar sources of the 'traditionally recognised' flowers such as hawthorn, which are usually considered to be vital to saproxylic invertebrates - Chatsworth could thus be an important site in research into the relationship between the invertebrates and their nectar sources.

In terms of future conservation, Chatsworth is in the enviable position of having a history of new oak plantings to supplement the existing ancient trees. This allays the common concern about imminent breaks in the continuity of availability of appropriate habitat for the fauna.

Table 1: Some of the invertebrate species found at Chatsworth.

Common name	Family	Species	Status	Description
A shining fungus beetle	Scaphidiidae	Scaphisoma agaricinum	Local	Small beetle found in fungi, usually in woodland.
A rove beetle	Staphylinidae	Lathrobium pallidum	pRDBK	A reddish rove beetle of uncertain ecology, found in litter, grass tussocks, etc. Very local in southern England.
Rhinoceros Beetle	Lucanidae	Sinodendron cylindricum	Common	Rhinoceros beetle. Larvae bore into firm dead timber of broadleaved trees in early stages of decay. Widespread but local. Occurs in most ancient woodlands but also common in secondary woods, old trees in hedges, etc.
Brown Chafer	Scarabaeidae	Serica brunnea	Local	A brown chafer, about 10mm long, occurring sandy and chalky areas. Can be found at exuding sap. Flies at night and is often attracted to lights.
A net-winged beetle	Lycidae	Pyropterus nigroruber	Na	Conspicuous scarlet and black beetle. Larvae in dead wood. Restricted to old woodlands around Nottinghamshire, Lincolnshire and Yorkshire. Adults often found in numbers on bracken.
Cobweb Beetle	Dermestidae	Ctesias serra	Notable/Nb	Small oval brown beetle living on dry remains of insects caught in spider webs under very dry bark, mainly in old woodland. Very local in S England, becoming rare in the N.
Death Watch Beetle	Anobiidae	Xestobium rufovillosum	Common	Common species in southern England, indoors (where it can be very destructive pest) and in dead wood. Much more stenotypic in dry dead wood of very old trees in old woodland in the north, where it also less common as a pest species.
A wood boring beetle	Anobiidae	Dorcatoma chrysomelina	Local	Wood boring beetle found in decaying deciduous timber. England and Wales N to Scottish border.
A wood boring beetle	Anobiidae	Dorcatoma flavicornis	Notable/Nb	Small wood boring beetle found in rotten wood in old woodland. England S to Yorks.
A wood boring beetle	Anobiidae	Anitys rubens	Notable/Nb	Small wood boring beetle found in dead oak. England N to Yorks. Rare.
A domed fungus beetle	Peltidae	Thymalus limbatus	Notable/Nb	A domed bronze-brown beetle found under dry dead bark, usually of very old trees in old woodland. Widely distributed throughout Great Britain but restricted by habitat.
A timber beetle	Lymexylidae	Hylecoetus dermestoides	Notable/Nb	Large brown beetle, larvae in dead or unhealthy but not rotten wood. Adults swarm around trees, especially at dusk. Widespread, particularly in N and W, but restricted to old woodland.
A narrow bark beetle	Rhizophagidae	Rhizophagus ferrugineus	Local	A small red 'bark' beetle. Mainly found under old dead bark of broad-leaved and conifer timber, in fungi on dead wood and occasionally in wasps nests. Locally common in old woodland.
A narrow bark beetle	Rhizophagidae	Rhizophagus nitidulus	Notable/Nb	A small beetle found under dead bark of broad leaved and coniferous trees, and in fungus. Widespread throughout Great Britain but always rare.
A silken fungus beetle	Cryptophagidae	Cryptophagus micaceus	pRDBK	A beetle which occurs in the nests of tree-living wasps, especially hornets (*Vespa crabro*) though also recorded in a fungus on beech (*Fagus sylvatica*), at a *Cossus*-oak and off oak (*Quercus*). Adults: July to November. Very local, with few records, in S. Hants, Surrey and Berks.
A shiny fungus beetle	Erotylidae	Dacne bipustulata	Local	Small beetle tunnelling in bracket fungi on broad leaved trees, mainly in old woodland. Commoner in the south.
A cerylonid beetle	Cerylonidae	Cerylon ferrugineum	Local	A small red beetle living under dead bark of deciduous trees. Very common in southern England but indicative of old woodland in the North.
A mould beetle	Lathridiidae	Aridius bifasciatus	Naturalised	1.5-2mm long mottled brown beetle found in leaf litter, compost, grass tussocks etc. Introduced and now one of the commonest species of beetle in Britain.
A mould beetle	Lathridiidae	Enicmus rugosus	Notable/Nb	A widely distributed but uncommon plaster beetle, found in fungi on trees or under bark.
A mould beetle	Lathridiidae	Corticaria longicollis	pRDBK	A small beetle found in ancient, broad-leaved woodland (grade 1 indicated species: Harding and Rose, 1986). Ecology uncertain as it has been found in a red-rotten hollow oak and in the nest of the wood ant, *Formica rufa*. Adults: March In myxomycete fungi (slime-moulds) mainly on pine (*Pinus*) trees. and July. Widespread but very rare, being recorded on very few occasions, though recently in two localities.
A small fungus beetle	Cisidae	Cis vestitus	Local	Small fungus beetle found in bracket fungi, particularly on oak in old woodland. Widespread but very local.
A hairy fungus beetle	Mycetophagidae	Triphyllus bicolor	Local	3-4mm long black beetle with red bases to the elytra. Lives in fungi on dead wood. Widespread but local, mainly in older woodland.
A hairy fungus beetle	Mycetophagidae	Mycetophagus piceus	Notable/Nb	Small beetle found under fungus infected bark and in bracket fungi on broad leaved timber. Restricted to old woodland. England S to Yorks.
A hairy fungus beetle	Mycetophagidae	Mycetophagus quadripustulatus	Local	Black and orange beetle living in bracket fungi and under bark, often congregating in large numbers with other members of the genus. Locally common throughout England and Wales, often in old woodland but frequently in isolated unhealthy trees.

Table 1 continued.

Common name	Family	Species	Status	Description
A narrow timber beetle	Colydiidae	*Bitoma crenata*	Local	Beetle found under bark of fungus infected wood, particularly oak. Indicative of old woodland, particularly so in the N.
A darkling beetle	Tenebrionidae	*Cylindrinotus laevioctostriatus*	Common	10-15mm dark bronze/brown "darkling" beetle. Specialist nocturnal grazer of *Pleurococcus* algae on tree bark, also grazing lichens on heather to access the algae. Often found under bark, or among heather litter during the day. Habitats include woodland, heathland and coastal cliffs. Widely distributed, common in S England, becoming much more local northwards and westwards.
A false darkling beetle	Melandryidae	*Orchesia undulata*	Local	A small saltatory beetle living in fungi, mainly in brackets but also under fungus infested bark. Widely distributed, mainly in older woodland.
A false darkling beetle	Melandryidae	*Conopalpus testaceus*	Notable/Nb	A beetle found under the bark of dead tree branches. This species is restricted to England and Wales.
A longhorn beetle	Cerambycidae	*Alosterna tabacicolor*	Local	Small yellow longhorn beetle. Larvae in rotting wood/stumps of broad leaved trees. Adults on flowers. Common in S and W becoming rare in the N.
Tanbark Borer	Cerambycidae	*Phymatodes testaceus*	Local	Very variable longhorn beetle, both in size and colour, red to metallic blue. Southern species, very uncommon in the north. Dead wood, particularly oak.
A longhorn beetle	Cerambycidae	*Leiopus nebulosus*	Local	Small ash grey and brown longhorn beetle. Larvae in dead wood. Common in S. England, local in the north where it is more strongly associated with old woodland.
A longhorn beetle	Cerambycidae	*Saperda scalaris*	Na	Spectacular yellow/green and black mottled longhorn beetle breeding in dead wood and under bark of most species of broadleaved trees, adults feeding on tree leaves. Northern species. Very local.
A longhorn beetle	Cerambycidae	*Stenostola dubia*	Notable/Nb	Small, bluish longhorn beetle. Larvae in dead wood of deciduous trees, particularly lime. Southern species.
A bark or ambrosia beetle	Scolytidae	*Scolytus intricatus*	Local	Bark beetle found on Oak and other deciduous trees.
A bark or ambrosia beetle	Scolytidae	*Dryocoetinus villosus*	Local	A local 'bark' beetle. Larvae bore into the wood of oak, beech and chestnut.
A bark or ambrosia beetle	Scolytidae	*Ernoporus caucasicus*	RDB1	A small bark beetle which lives in the bark of dead, thick branches of limes (*Tilia* spp.). It is known from a very few midlands sites, but may be under-recorded.
Clouded Magpie	Geometridae	*Abraxas sylvata*	Local	Inhabits woodland and parkland, the larva feeding on *Ulmus*. Local over much of Britain, ranging north to Dumfriesshire.
Alder Kitten	Notodontidae	*Furcula bicuspis*	Notable/Nb	Inhabits woodland, the larva feeding on *Betula* and *Alnus*. Local, southern half of England, south-east Wales, Norfolk and parts of the Midlands.
Muslin Footman	Arctiidae	*Nudaria mundana*	Local	The larva feeds on various lichens growing on stone walls, fences and bushes. Locally in many parts of the British Isles as far north as Aberdeenshire.
A hoverfly	Syrphidae	*Didea intermedia*	Notable/Nb	Black and orange hoverfly. Little is known about its habitat requirements but larvae predatory on aphids on pine. Widespread, but most reliable records are from the Scottish Highlands - misidentifications are probably frequent.
A hoverfly	Syrphidae	*Brachypalpoides lenta*	Local	Conspicuous red and black hoverfly of old woodland. Larvae in rotten wood, usually in hollows in live trees, especially beech. Very local, mainly in S England. Scattered populations N to Highland.
A hoverfly	Syrphidae	*Brachypalpus laphriformis*	Notable/Nb	A scarce hoverfly which mimics a hive bee. Ancient woods, mainly recorded from southern England but with scattered colonies further north and in Wales. The larvae occur dead wood, particularly standing hollow trunks of beech and ash when these are broken off 2-4 metres above the ground.
A hoverfly	Syrphidae	*Xylota sylvarum*	Local	Dead wood hoverfly. Common in S England becoming rarer in the north. Larvae under rotten bark and have been recorded as breeding in sawdust piles.
Marble Gall	Cynipidae	*Andricus kollari*	Unknown	Common, frequently abundant. Agamic gall on *Quercus robur* and *Q. petraea* single, sometimes coalescent, up to 20mm diameter pale green, dark green, brownish yellow, reddish brown, vi onwards, mature ix; larvae solitary or gregarious. Sexual gall conglomerated on axillary buds of *Quercus cerris*, generally gregarious. Flight period: ix-x (agamic),v-vi(sexual).
A spider-hunting wasp	Pompilidae	*Dipogon variegatus*	Local	A spider hunting wasp. Very local.
Slender Bodied Digger Wasp	Sphecidae	*Crabro cribrarius*	Local	A large yellow and black solitary wasp which nests in sandy soil. Burrows are stocked with flies. Flies from a wide variety of families including Therevidae, Asilidae, Empididae, Syrphidae and Muscidae have been recorded as prey of this wasp. Widespread in open, sandy habitats in Britain north to Nairn and mid-Perthshire.
A solitary wasp	Sphecidae	*Crossocerus cetratus*	Local	Small black solitary wasp nesting in dead wood or sometimes in plant stems. Prey: small diptera and plant lice. Widespread throughout GB but very local.
A solitary wasp	Sphecidae	*Crossocerus binotatus*	Na	Yellow and black solitary wasp nesting in hard rotten wood, predatory on flies of the genus *Rhagio*. Widespread N to Scottish border counties but everywhere very local.
A solitary wasp	Sphecidae	*Rhopalum clavipes*	Local	Small (4-6mm), shiny black solitary wasp nesting in plant stems or, occasionally, holes in dead wood, mortar or sand. Prey chiefly Psocids, but also small Diptera and Homoptera (Aphids and Psyllids). Widespread and not uncommon.

The disparkment of medieval parks

Robert Liddiard
University of East Anglia

Abstract

The subject of disparkment has received relatively little attention from landscape historians. The origin and development of parkland in the Middle Ages remain topics for debate and reassessment but the processes by which medieval deer enclosures declined and were broken up are poorly understood. This paper offers a general commentary on the nature of disparkment in the post-medieval landscape. Incidents of disparkment can be found throughout the Middle Ages, but levels of disparkment rose in the late sixteenth century and during the Interregnum. However, the most decisive period of disparkment, appears to have been the early to mid eighteenth century, a time that saw large numbers of medieval parks broken up and either turned over to arable or retained as pasture.

Although the subject is one that requires a good deal of new research in order to bring out its full complexity at a local and regional level, some general factors behind the motivation for disparkment can be identified. Of some importance, however, is the need to differentiate between disparkment as a *process* and disparkment as an *event*. The process of disparkment could be a protracted affair. Indeed, when exactly a park was officially disparked is far from straightforward; an area could still be described as a 'park' and indeed retain a pale, when the enclosed area was farmed as individual fields and game no longer being managed within the bounds. Such a situation could persist for decades before the 'event' of breaking the pale took place and full disparkment occurred.

A series of interlinked factors appear to have been responsible for the final phase of disparkment in the eighteenth century. The decline of venison as an elite foodstuff and its replacement by other forms of game meant that the need for specific deer enclosures diminished and the cost of maintaining old parks inconvenient. Developments in the landscape setting of the noble mansion also played their part. By the mid eighteenth century, it was no longer felt necessary that those parks that surrounded the country house should contain deer. This was a change that again made the maintenance of deer enclosures increasingly irrelevant. At the same time, the series of changes associated with the Agricultural Revolution meant that the perceived marginal land that medieval parks frequently occupied could be cultivated and improved in ways that had hitherto not been possible. However, underpinning all these changes, was an ideological shift that was probably more significant in bringing about disparkment. Deer parks reflected a particular, and distinctly medieval, attitude to the elite landscape and the production of high status foodstuffs. It was this medieval regime of management that was increasingly perceived as illogical and without reason in the age of agricultural 'improvement'.

The eighteenth century is sometimes characterised as a period that witnessed the triumph of the park. However, it was also the time that saw the widespread removal of what for many centuries had been important elements in the social landscape of medieval and early post-medieval England.

The social impact of park-making in the Middle Ages

Stephen A Mileson
Oxford University

Abstract

There has been a good deal of interesting recent work on what may have attracted medieval lords to make parks, including explorations of these reserves as status-symbols which helped give their owners a sense of identity as well as providing hunting opportunities and secure supplies of wood and pasture. But less has been said about the possible effects of park-making on others - how their activities may have impacted upon neighbouring lords and wider communities. Indeed, it has justly been commented that the effect of medieval parks on local economies and populations is still 'largely unknown'. Yet, as new and very visible assertions of control over woods and pastures, parks seem to have interfered with established rights of use and access: in particular, they often appear to have restricted aristocrats and ordinary people from hunting and from exercising long-held 'common rights' of grazing and wood-gathering. And if parks really were status-symbols, it seems likely that their creation sometimes disrupted the established 'landscape of lordship' in certain localities, particularly where other lords had previously claimed exclusive hunting rights in their own chases or parks. At any rate, park-making seems to have been contentious, with new imparkments eliciting opposition and even violent action from lords and peasants alike. All this suggests that park creation ought to be explored as part of wider movements to define and delimit property rights and access to space. Since parks enclosed around a quarter of all woodland by the early 14th century, they deserve an important place in our understanding of what has recently been dubbed 'the 13th century enclosure movement', which took place during the high medieval period of growing population and pressure on resources, as well as in the very different period of enclosure which characterised the period of declining population after the Black Death.

The aim of this paper was to offer an outline of the main ways in which park creation affected landed and agricultural interests, and, just as significantly, how new parks may have challenged the existing social order in particular localities. The way in which lords and peasants responded to imparkment was explored through an examination of negotiations and legal actions as well as cases of violence and apparent direct action. An attempt was made to understand how reactions to parks may have been shaped by cultural and social values as well by purely pragmatic economic or agrarian considerations. The similarities and differences in the issues posed by park creation and the responses to it in the periods before and after the Black Death was also considered.

Aerial view of the de la Beche family's park at La Beche (near Aldworth), Berkshire, licensed in 1335.

Medieval Parks in Yorkshire: Range and Content

Stephen Moorhouse

Abstract

This paper will summarize the results of thirty years work on the form, function and contents of medieval parks in Yorkshire. The approach has been from the discipline of the landscape historian, using primarily a wide variety of documents (particularly the '*costs of the park*' section of manorial accounts) and map sources, minor name evidence, and (by far the more enlightening) large area detailed field survey.

It is clear that parks at all levels of the aristocracy had many uses, and the term '*deer park*' is most misleading. Above all, it narrows our view of medieval parks and more importantly the wide range of uses and the physical remains that those uses have left in the earthwork landscape. The term '*park*' is to be preferred.

Indeed a wide range of features are documented in parks dealing with many aspects of their economy. A selected range of features from many to be considered includes: the home park, rabbit warrens, gardens, kennels, many types of animal traps (many made from rope), towers for various functions, horse studs, cattle farms, sheephouse complexes, and, where parks overlie mineral deposits, often extensive coal mining, iron mining and smelting and stone quarrying.

This abstract summarizes a paper in Robert Liddiard (Ed.) *The Medieval Park: New Perspectives* (Windgather Press, 2007), which was launched at the Conference.

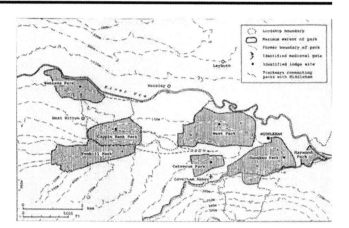

Figure 1

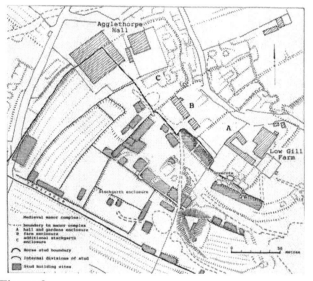

Figure 2

'The king's chief delights': visits to royal deer parks in the later Middle Ages

Amanda Richardson

University of Chichester/ University of Winchester

Abstract

The great royal deer parks of the Middle Ages are arguably among our earliest examples of designed landscapes, and most remain very prominent in the English countryside. Yet little detailed attention has been given to the way their inner landscapes may have functioned. This paper will redress the balance by considering the role of parkland as a backdrop to key residences of the Crown, and by problematising the seasonality of royal visits.

Aside from noting the main Christian festivals, historians of medieval palaces have not explicitly taken into account the timing of royal visits. Yet a consideration of seasonality, applied to royal landscapes, not only adds to our understanding of the creation and consolidation of later medieval social relationships centred on the hunt, but might also enhance our perception of attendant changes in the design and use of medieval elite landscapes. For example, shifts in the timing of royal trips to Clarendon Palace (Wilts.) and its park apparently calibrate literary evidence concerning changes in hunting practice in the later Middle Ages. That is, through the twelfth and thirteenth centuries the court usually visited in winter, when does were almost certainly hunted. However, fourteenth-century kings seem to have preferred high summer, when bucks would have been the quarry.

It is in fact possible to posit the fourteenth century as the great age of deer parks, at least from the perspective of the English crown, and to see similarities in 'design' with the narratives of contemporary literary and prescriptive tracts. However such sources play an increasing role in the reconstruction of past landscapes, and perhaps we too readily assume that the ideal invariably became reality, consequently reading too much purpose into relict landscape features. With this in mind, questions addressed in this paper were those recently advocated for the study of late medieval parks generally. How many royal parks actually surrounded (or were adjacent to) key buildings? Do they appear to have been deliberately laid out in order to offset those residences, and can chronological relationships between the two be discerned? Results show that English kings preferred their residences to be surrounded by 'parkscapes'. If parks were some distance away, new ones were created nearby, as at Windsor, or lodges might be set up within them, as at Guildford (Surrey). As to whether parks were designed in tandem with buildings at the instigation of particular lords, Edward II was almost certainly behind the creation of Clarendon Park (Wilts) at its greatest 4,292-acre extent, at the same time as the palace was improved to provide a fitting venue for a parliament. Similarly, the hand of Edward III is discernible in the foundation of Windsor Little Park as a setting for his revamped castle.

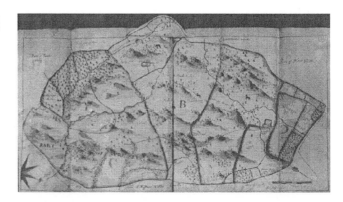

John Norden's 1607 plan of Windsor Great Park. 1142252 Table IV, 'The great park'. The Royal Collection © 2006 Her Majesty Queen Elizabeth II

The ecology and economics of Medieval deer parks

Ian D. Rotherham
Sheffield Hallam University

Summary

Where deer parks survive, and even this is rare, they do so as a unique landscape separated in time and function from their origins. They reflect the landscapes of the time and place they were imparked and the changes in economic function and ecology over a long lifespan. The ecologies of these landscapes were driven by uses in a multi-functional system of economic utilisation. As purpose changed so did ecology, each new phase incorporating, preserving, or removing those that preceded it. It is argued by Frans Vera (Vera, 2000), that these are landscapes that originate in medieval or earlier times, and give a unique insight into once great primeval savannah across much of northwestern Europe. Certainly, their remarkable biodiversities provide evidence of such potential lineage. These landscapes present palimpsests of ecology and archaeology that reflect their economically driven origins over 800-1,200 years.

There is a wealth of literature on a diversity of aspects of medieval parks, from their invertebrate ecologies, to rare lichens and bryophytes, to their herds of deer, their fishponds, and to the politics of fashion and taste and the provision of sport and entertainment for an affluent elite. This is a far greater literature than can be the focus of this paper, although much more is covered in the other papers of this volume. However, it is clear that there is still a need for more multi-disciplinary meetings such as the conference held at Sheffield Hallam University in September 2007. Very often each specialist group has its own meetings and produces its own literature, each excellent in its own sphere, but crying out for these riches to be brought together in one place. Some key aspects of forests and chases are brought together in Langton & Jones (2005), and many of these relate to early parks too. Paul Warde in that volume notes how fuel uses and its economy for example, are neglected fields of historical research. The same oversight applies to parklands, which driven by economy and politics have acquired a uniquely rich ecology and a heritage interest, that are both steeped in history. To more fully understand and appreciate the wildlife and heritage of the medieval parks we must consider not only their ecology, but also the social drivers behind their origins and their survival. Their study crosses to that of other recreational, hunting, and productive landscapes such as chases, forests, wooded commons, and wastes. In particular, with the emphasis on *deer* parks, we must also look to literature on hunting (e.g. Blüchel, 1997) and associated activities such as falconry. With the food production aspect of the park, it is useful to consider literature on warrens (e.g. Henderson, 1997; Williamson, 2006) and fishponds for example.

An Introduction to Parks and their Ecology

Since Oliver Rackham's seminal works *Ancient Woodland* (1980) and *The History of the Countryside* (1986), it has been clear that wood-pasture was once the most abundant type of wooded landscape in northwestern Europe. In essence, wood-pasture is a system of land management where trees are grown, but grazing by large herbivores is also permitted by domesticated, semi-domesticated, wild, or a combination of stock. Wood-pasture in England is well documented for over one thousand years, and *Domesday Book* (1086) probably records a landscape dominated by the practice. It has been suggested that wood-pasture was an ancient system of management that developed in a multi-functional landscape where woodland was plentiful and where there was little need for formal coppice. The latter is a more intensive and rigorously managed system, intended to ensure vital supplies of wood and timber in a resource-limited landscape (Fowler, 2002; Hayman, 2003; Perlin, 1989). Pasture-woodland is an older (and in many ways, system that is more 'natural'). Significantly, most livestock, wild or domesticated, will take leaf fodder or browse, if offered, in preference to grazing (Vera, 2000).

Medieval parks are part of a suite of landscape types that mix trees and grazing or browsing mammals. These include wood-pasture, wooded commons, forests, the relicts of what was probably in prehistory a great wooded savannah across much of northwestern Europe. In both origins and ecology parks as essentially a form of 'pasture-woodland',

related to forests, heaths, moors, and some commons, with grazing animals and variable tree cover. Aside from the obvious external enclosure, these landscapes are often essentially unenclosed grazing lands. In considering their ecology, it is important to establish origins and relationships to other wildlife habitats.

The idea and techniques of constructing and maintaining a park to keep animals such as deer long pre-dates the Norman Conquest; parks being known from the first century BC in both Roman Italy and Gaul. Cummins (1998) notes a document of Charlemagne from 812 AD that clearly refers to the maintenance of a hunting park and its boundary. The dates of establishment and the numbers of parks in England remain a matter of debate. There is evidence at Conisbrough Castle Park, South Yorkshire for example, of a possible lineage of enclosure from around 600-700 AD (Paul Buckland and Colin Merrony pers. comm.). However, the functions are not confirmed and the locations of earlier and medieval features are displaced. Liddiard (2003) presents an overview of parks in the context of *Domesday Book*, drawing attention to the possible similarity between parks and hays; the latter being rather enigmatic and perhaps representing a variety of hunting structures with differing degrees of permanence.

In the two centuries following the Norman Conquest, numbers of parks in England increased dramatically to perhaps 3,000, with possibly fifty in Wales, and eighty in Scotland. From the early thirteenth century, a royal licence was technically necessary to create a

park in areas of royal forest; though Cummins (1988) notes that in both England and Scotland baronial parks were also created without licence. Where documents survive, they provide invaluable reference materials for a now vanished age, giving insight into landscape and ecology. The average English medieval park was around 100 acres, although size could vary considerably. The date of establishment, the area enclosed, the functions of the park and the interplay between enclosed and unenclosed areas all influence the ecology of these landscapes (Jones, 1996; Jones *et al.*, 1996).

Ancient Wooded Landscapes

In Britain, there are two broad distinctions in 'ancient woodland' landscapes. Firstly, there are coppice woods, often managed since the medieval period as simple coppice, or more frequently 'coppice-with-standards'. Such areas have relatively few large trees, but strikingly rich and sometimes diverse ground floras. Secondly, there are parklands, which may have historic links back to their use as medieval parks. These areas generally have poorer ground floras due to grazing livestock, and are characterised by massive and ancient trees, chiefly 'pollards'. In terms of wildlife conservation, it has been assumed that coppice woods were excellent habitat for woodland birds and flowers and parks for rare lichens and fungi growing on the trees, and insects or other invertebrates that depended on veteran tree dead wood habitat. The general assumption was that coppice woods had strong links to ancient landscapes and vaguely conceptualised 'wildwood' (Beswick and Rotherham, 1993).

Research over the last twenty years has shown many of these assumptions incorrect or naïve in their interpretation. Researchers such as Paul Harding developed interest in British pasture-woodlands, and Frans Vera has challenged many accepted 'truths' of woodland history, placing park landscapes in their wider ecological context. Much current excitement about deer park landscape ecology is because they appear to represent the closest analogies to northwestern European primeval forest landscapes. Parks are juxtaposed with, but

different from, medieval coppice woods. They are unique resources for conservation; providing insights into ecological history (Rollins, 2003). Research by scholars such as Keith Alexander and Roger Key have transformed the understanding of the importance of parks for invertebrates, and Ted Green has awakened interest in ancient tree fungi and the significance of the trees themselves. In northern Britain, Chris Smout (2003), and others have transformed our knowledge of Scottish woods and the Caledonian Pine Forests and palaeo-ecologists such as Paul Buckland have closed gaps in information concerning these landscapes and their ecologies in prehistoric and more recent periods.

Recent studies are drawn together by seminal writings of authorities like Oliver Rackham (1976), George Peterken (1981 and 1996), and Donald Pigott (1993) to forge coherent visions of woodland landscape ecology, with parks representing an important component. It is of significance that until relatively recently medieval parks were not considered by conservation agencies to be 'ancient woodland', and so seemed to be the 'Cinderellas' of nature conservation. From a broader 'woodland' perspective, it is possible to assess the historical ecology of medieval parks and to attempt to place them in their landscape context. Parks have trees (usually but not always), and large (and sometimes smaller) grazing mammals, and to survive trees need protection. Some parkland trees are ornamental and others are managed '*working*' trees, with fundamental differences in species and structures associated with these different functions. Taigel & Williamson (1993) and Bettey (1993) give useful introductions to the complexities of these landscapes. Such historical contributions are important since the ecologists must understand history, and the historian the ecosystem. The potential of cross-fertilisation is considerable: Rackham (2004) provides an eloquent exposition on the evolution of park landscapes and of their trees in particular, and Muir (2005) is a particularly accessible account of recent developments.

The Parkland Palimpsest

It is necessary to differentiate medieval parks from other imparked areas and from other associated grazing landscapes, a process that can often be difficult. Indeed as other papers in this volume demonstrate, there are major differences of opinion and hence difficulties in defining exactly what a park was or is. Parks share features with other unenclosed grazed landscapes with trees and woods, such as chases, forests, moors, and heaths. A complicating factor is that many parks took in significant elements of earlier landscapes when they were enclosed often from 'waste' or 'forest'. In some cases, park management has allowed parts of this ancient ecology to survive or, in other cases, parks include features from periods of positive management with specific ends and outcomes, followed by abandonment, or changed use. Each phase will necessarily preserve, modify, or remove the earlier ecology of working landscapes that have sometimes evolved over a thousand years or more. To understand today's ecology requires awareness of changes through both management and neglect. Imparkment may have affected the original ecology in different ways:

1) **Preservation**: original features and species maintained within the enclosed area.
2) **Modification**: original features and species maintained but modified within the enclosed area.
3) **Removal and replacement**: original features and species removed by enclosure and subsequent management, to be replaced by new features and a new ecology.

Such processes may have occurred during the original establishment of an early park or at each subsequent phase of 'improvement' or abandonment, generating both continuity and innovation. Such a process varies from site to site, in some cases all that remains is a single veteran tree or it may be a significant parkland resource with substantial elements from earlier periods. Trelowarren Park on the Lizard remains as an intact boundary with mature trees and an ancient woodland flora; yet the parkland core has long since gone, replaced by

agricultural fields. According to Pett (1998), it was disparked before 1736 when Tonkin described it as '*long since disparked*'. Charles Henderson the Cornish historian writing in the early 1900s, noted that '*The site is not known but there is a part of the demesne called the Warren*'. Old trees on the park pale are not veteran park trees, but hedgerow trees since grown out. Earthworks and differences in vegetation may be evidence of changed land-use and boundaries, with a 'ha ha' being dug in the early 1800s to form a boundary between the estate and the unenclosed moorland of Goohhilly Down (Pett, 1998). In a similar vein, at Calke Abbey in Derbyshire for example, the present-day park includes large areas of former medieval open fields, with their characteristic sinuous ridges and furrows. Other parks incorporate short, straight ridge and furrow from Napoleonic or Victorian steam-plough incursions into the park landscape during the late eighteenth and nineteenth centuries.

There is a clear problem in that ecological research has often failed to differentiate between different origins and histories. For many ecologists, a park is a park. The reality is very different and consequently the study of ecology in parks is often not set within a reliable historical framework. There is also little hard information on the ecology of these landscapes in previous periods when they were 'functioning' parks. For such evidence, assumptions are often made retrospectively, based on modern observations. Either that or they are gleaned from material such as household and estate accounts. The complexity of park occurrence and presentation in the landscape, both today and in the past, is illustrated by Squires and Humphrey (1986), investigating and mapping in detail the parks of the former Charnwood Forest, Leicestershire. To understand the historical ecology of parks, it is essential to appreciate their form and function, and how these have changed over time. In many cases, only a fragment of the earlier landscape is visible today, and sometimes these fragments remain unrecognised. Even where a park survives with proven continuity to earlier periods, however, the management today will differ from the past. Whilst the former ecology, or the management that maintained it, may not be fully understood, it is known that the two were inextricably linked. That park management, the wider landscape in which it is seated and specific features within it will have fluxed greatly over what is often a long history, is not in doubt. The ecology of today reflects this part continuum and part palimpsest. As Squires & Humphrey (1986) suggest, the appreciation of any particular park requires consideration of form and function, and the context of the development of the manor as a whole. Such thinking applies to a park's ecology as it does to other aspects of the landscape.

The Uses and Functions of Medieval Parks

Cantor (Squires & Humphrey, 1986) notes that the medieval park was an important feature in its landscape. He emphasises, however, how the medieval park was different in character to its modern counterpart, the latter based on images of eighteenth- or nineteenth-century landscaped parks, or of nineteenth- or twentieth-century municipal parks. As Cantor notes, medieval parks were very different, often areas of rough, uncultivated landscape, usually wooded, and frequently on the edge of manors away from cultivation (Cantor & Hatherly, 1979). Owned by the lord of the manor, these were designed as hunting parks, stocked with deer and other game, and providing food and sport in varying balance. Our vision of a working medieval park is in a landscape of open field, waste, woodland, and royal forest, with their ecologies inexorably linked.

Medieval parks provided hunting, foodstuffs, and wood and timber for building and fuel. Alongside deer, medieval parks contained wild boar, hares, rabbits (reintroduced to Britain by the Normans), game birds, fish in fishponds, together with grazing for cattle and sheep. In the case of parks such as Bradgate, pannage (feeding pigs on acorns) from the oaks provided revenue in rents. Parks generally had large areas of heath or grassland (called launds or plains) dotted with trees, along with

woodlands (called holts or coppices, and if for holly (*Ilex aquifolium*) hollins). The launds and the coppices provided food for animals in summer, and in the case of hollins, through the winter months. The park may have held and maintained deer (fallow (*Dama dama*), and red (*Cervus elaphus*)) for the table and for the hunt. In the latter case, this sometimes involved release beyond the park pale and into the chase beyond (Whitehead 1964 and 1980). Cummins (1988) discusses the size of parks and the differences between smaller baronial parks with semi-domesticated animals, and the much larger royal parks. Some parks extended over many miles, Woodstock (Oxon.) had a perimeter of seven miles and permitted hunting on a grand scale. Others were much smaller, with some little more than deer paddocks. It follows that their ecologies must have been similarly varied with larger parks able to maintain more of the earlier wilderness and the associated ecology. There were also links between both hunting in parks and in the forest or chase beyond, and in their ecologies. Alongside deer, other livestock exerted additional grazing pressures, with, for example, specific areas set aside, enclosed, and maintained as rabbit warrens. The extent and influence of parks could be substantial and beyond one individual site: according to Cummins (1988) in 1512, the Earls of Northumberland had 5,571 deer in twenty-one parks spread across Northumberland, Cumberland, and Yorkshire.

Solitary trees in the launds were pollarded (high coppice), and some shredded (branches removed from the tall, main stem). The only new tree growth outside the woods took place in the protection of thickets of hawthorn (*Crataegus monogyna*), holly, and bramble (*Rubus fruticosus* agg.). There were special woods called holly hags or hollins where holly cut on rotation fed the deer in winter. A boundary fence, called the park pale; a cleft oak fence, or a bank with a cleft oak fence, or a wall, surrounded the park. If there was a bank, it normally had an internal ditch. Park pales often contained structures called *deer leaps* to entice wild deer into the park. Buildings in parks included manor houses (from Tudor times), keepers' lodges, and banqueting houses. The park was multi-functional and part of the wider economy of the manor. Turf and stone were extracted, mineral coal too if it occurred. Squires and Humphrey (1986) noted arable crops such as cereals grown within the park pale. Deer were a priority but shared the landscape with other domestic stock such as cattle, horses, and even goats. The park at Wharncliffe Chase near Sheffield even acquired North American Buffalo in the early twentieth century (Jones and Jones 2005). Many parks such as at Wharncliffe near Sheffield had warrens within them or close by and relict 'pillow mounds' and other features may now evidence these.

Other parks had productive fishponds that may survive today as ornamental features, but more often are abandoned, frequently obscure complexes of shallow pools and channels for an early industrial farming of fish (mostly carp), for the table. An anonymous monk wrote in 1468 '*The mill pond. And in the seven year of the king, twenty-eighth day of January, I brake mine greatest pond in the park, and out of that I took great breams, sixty-five. And put them into the mill pond the which is new made; and I put the same day in to the same pond six great carps and ... little carps twelve score.*' (Fagan, 2006). In most medieval parks that have survived through the landscape period until today, the water features are often highly modified for ornament, and may bear little resemblance and often have no link to the productive medieval ponds.

With socio-economic changes, the fashions for parks and the means for their upkeep fluctuated. Most deer parks were created from 1200 to 1350. They then declined following the impact of the Black Death (Mileson, 2005). Subsequently, boundaries moved, and small parks were enlarged or replaced by new creations. Parks and their relationship to great houses also changed with time and fashion. Originally an enclosed area at a small distance from the main house, perhaps containing hunting lodges later parks were increasingly the settings for houses and gardens. The house

moved to the park, or the park was moved or modified to envelop the house. Expensive and difficult to maintain, many deer parks fell from fashion, abandoned and destroyed. Between the fifteenth and eighteenth centuries, medieval deer parks were deliberately removed (disparkment), to become large, compartmented coppice woods, or farmland. As the rural economy changed so did the values and costs of a park. Many were abandoned during the English Civil War (1642-1649), and few survived intact as the wave of agricultural improvement swept through the landscape from 1600 onwards. Some such as Tinsley Park in Sheffield, and Tankersley Park in Barnsley, were lost to industrial development as landowners discovered coal and ironstone beneath their land. A small number retained their medieval character, and some of their functions to the present day.

Park Ecology

The ecology of working parks reflects the factors described above. What survives today mirrors these events and pressures. Park landscapes had unimproved grassland across much of the grazed area, species and communities varying with grazing intensity. Many grassland plants and associated invertebrates cannot cope with short swards and intensive grazing. However, if grazing levels were low or areas seasonally protected from livestock, the vegetation would grow tall, flower and set seed; similar to modern unimproved pasture and hay meadow. Such areas would be rich in wild flowers and in associated invertebrates such as butterflies, bees, and hoverflies. They would be part of a patchwork of shorter grass, bare ground, and in acidic locations, heath. Wet areas such as valley bottoms, or land with impeded drainage, had extensive moist grassland, marsh or bog. The typical plants of ancient woodlands (such as dog's mercury (*Mercurialis perennis*), wood anemone (*Anemone nemorosa*), primrose (*Primula vulgaris*), and bluebell (*Hyacinthoides non-scripta*)) would have been restricted and found only in enclosed woods, copses, lane sides, hedgerows, or streamsides, and perhaps in areas of less intensive grazing.

Keystone species in the park were deer, with other grazing mammals of varying domestication; these animals being the main drivers in the deer park ecosystem. Other important ecological components were fungi in the unimproved grasslands, and associated with extensive animal dunging. There would have been a rich fungal flora of both mycorrhizal associates of both trees (ectomycorrhizas), and of grasses and forbes in the sward (vesicular-arbuscular mycorrhizas). These would present as both individual groups of toadstool fruiting bodies as can be seen today with the dung-associated species such as the shaggy ink caps (*Coprinus* sp.), and as spectacular '*fairy rings*'. Associated with animal dunging would be rich faunas of coprophagous and predatory flies, and dung beetles. It can be assumed that high numbers of animals would lead to carcases and faunas of species such as burying beetles. With the high numbers of mammals were rich faunas of parasites such as mites, ticks, and biting or egg-laying flies.

Imparking sometimes included deliberate or accidental preservation of domesticated, semi-domesticated, or wild grazing mammals within the enclosure. The white park cattle are a case in point, with the Chillingham Park herd in Northumberland perhaps the best example; aside from a small herd established some distance away as a precaution against foot-and-mouth disease, this unique breed of ancient cattle survives at only one location. Whitaker in 1892 described the park as 1,500 acres, well wooded, and with moor and wild grounds (Whitaker, 1892). This ancient and extensive park enclosed and encapsulated an entire ecosystem that has been maintained ever since, though with considerable modifications as described by Stephen Hall (this volume). Outside the park, species including the cattle have long since disappeared. Enclosure of large areas of semi-natural landscape was not the exclusive prerogative of the deer parks. Ornamental parks of the seventeenth and eighteenth century often involved similar scales of enclosure, sometimes from common fields but often from the 'waste'. This may have

included marshes, grasslands, heaths, and extensive bogs. Hotham and North Cave Park in the East Riding is such an example (Neave and Turnbull 1992). Management as a park also affected other species both within and beyond the pale. In particular, predators were vigorously controlled and this would have impacts on ecology that were deep and long lasting; the control of both foxes and wolves being noted in estate accounts.

Trees and Wood

The importance of ancient or old wood, living and dead or dying, standing or fallen, has been recognised over the previous two decades. Key publications (Read, 1999; Speight, 1989; Kirby & Drake 1993) have highlighted the role of wood for saproxylic invertebrates, especially insects. Others (Rose, 1974, 1976; Harding & Rose, 1986) have noted the habitat value for epiphytic plants, lichens, and fungi. A characteristic of most, but not all, parks were large, often very old, trees. In the best cases, these provide good quality saproxylic habitats and important continuity of resource over many centuries.

Park trees may have been a mixture of timber trees enclosed when the park was formed. Others were planted deliberately as part of the park management. Many parks such as Chatsworth in Derbyshire include later additions through the conversion of field systems and their hedgerow trees. These trees are now veterans in the contemporary landscape but originated in an agricultural environment. Most of the very old trees, often oak (*Quercus robur*), are specimens that have been actively managed for at least several centuries and then abandoned. Now ranging from youngsters of maybe 400 years, to real veterans of anything from 800 to 1,200 years, these specimen trees represent one of the most precious resources of former medieval parks. However, some parks known to be early established, such as Prideaux Place Park in Cornwall, are devoid of major veteran trees. It is possible that some parks never had them, or that they have been removed at some point in the park's long history. Early estate survey maps often record significant veteran trees which can be matched to the modern landscape. In other cases, removal is recorded in estate accounts. Younger veterans could be valuable timber trees taken in time of financial pressure. When the Duke of Newcastle's Clumber Park estate in Nottinghamshire was sold in the 1940s, the main interest was from local timber merchants who planned to remove all the veteran trees of any commercial value. The National Trust acquired the site and developed it as a recreational park, recouping some of their outlay from sale of large oaks from the park's ancient woods.

Large trees performed many functions in working parks, providing shelter in winter and shade in summer for cattle and deer. Importantly, they could also provide herbage to feed to the livestock; most deer and cattle preferring to browse on leaves and shoots, than graze grass. To ensure a continuous supply of branches and leaves, the trees were cut high, several metres above ground, keeping re-growth out of the reach of the grazing animals, until the parker cut it for fodder. The technique was known as pollarding and is in effect a high coppice. Furthermore, the provision of special hollins and hags ensured herbage was provided for livestock throughout the winter. For several months of the year, and longer during colder periods, grass does not grow in Britain and stock consequently depend on stores of hay, a valuable and often scarce commodity, and cut branches of evergreen holly. Pollarding extended the lifespan of trees beyond that normally achieved and in so doing ensured a major supply and continuity of dead wood, a highly important wildlife habitat.

Large oaks were grown for timber, in some cases, the trunks and boughs were carefully nurtured to form particular shapes and sizes for specific functions. Careful planning and management over many decades are key aspects of park historical ecology. The records of great estates often give precise details of the removal of trees, their price, and destination. Around the park, sometimes as individuals or as small groups, trees of a diversity of species, native and exotic, were planted. The form and

the species obviously varied with time and fashion. Now neglected, these younger veterans add to the resource of dead and dying wood in the contemporary park landscape.

Where air pollution allows, the bark of these great trees provides habitat for rare lichens. However, oaks have acidic bark, are relatively poor in lichens, and gross air pollution for over a century has exterminated many species over large areas especially the English lowlands. With air pollution falling, there has been a remarkable recovery in the lichen populations of many areas including the veteran trees of former medieval parks. The importance of ancient pasture woodlands for survival of rare epiphytic lichens was highlighted by Francis Rose and colleagues, and the recovery well documented by Oliver Gilbert (Rose, 1974, 1976; Rose & James, 1974; James *et al.*, 1977).

The Importance of Dead Wood and Continuity

Of all the ecological features of ancient parks, conservationists regard the veteran trees and their dead wood as the priority resource. EU regulations have targeted dead wood because of its associated unique and diverse fauna and flora and because habitat loss and modification has resulted in critically low levels across Europe. Dead and dying wood provide unique opportunities for specialist fungi, invertebrates, slime moulds, and birds such as woodpeckers, while hole-nesting species such as owls and bats benefit from veteran trees. The latter are specially protected under EU and UK legislation following dramatic declines over the last fifty years. Parkland, especially if it includes rivers and lakes, provide some of their best habitats.

The value of dead wood for wildlife varies with aspect, humidity, temperature, state of decay, continuity on site (as many associated species are highly immobile), and whether it is on living or dead trees. If dead, then whether the tree is standing or has fallen also affects associated ecology. Careful analysis of associated fauna and flora provides insights into ecological history, and former site management, with the potential to document an ecological archive to complement other sources of historical information. In particular, many associated species require habitat continuity over time, presence, or absence of key species giving information on site management and on significant breaks in parkland regimes.

Relationships between ancient woodland, especially pasture woods, and their saproxylic fauna are critical to understanding park historical ecology. Invertebrates vary dramatically in habitat requirements, and importantly here, in dispersal behaviour. Some species migrate, in many cases over considerable distances, and others disperse moderate distances from their breeding sites to new areas. A few species are very limited in their ability to move, and in a very few cases, at least under contemporary environmental conditions, means only a few metres from the trees from which they emerged. In most cases the larval stage lives in the dead wood or associated habitats, and the adult, perhaps a beetle or hoverfly emerges to disperse, breed and lay eggs. The critical habitat is the dead and dying wood of ancient parkland trees, but other environments and communities in the park matrix are also important. Adult insects such as hoverflies or beetles, may feed on nectar and pollen of plants such as bramble (*Rubus fruticosus*), or hogweed (*Heracleum sphondylium*), and require suitably mature plants in abundance with the right conditions of temperature and sunlight. Some ancient woodland indicators, for example certain hoverflies, feed not on dead wood itself but on abundant aphids associated with old trees. However, the hoverflies still seem to be closely associated with continuity of old trees on site. Of the dead wood specialists, some feed on the

wood itself in varying degrees of decay, others on the fungi that cause rot. For high-grade invertebrate faunas in these ancient habitats, the keys are habitat continuity and quality. Some species are very specific and in a few cases, like the black and yellow wasp mimic cranefly *Ctenophora flaveolata*, a Red Data Book species, dependent on soft, decaying heartwood of massive veteran beeches.

It is important to differentiate between species requiring dead wood habitats, and those that need continuity. This is because, as indicators, they tell different stories. Interpretation depends on assumptions about behavioural changes with climate fluctuations, many invertebrates dispersing more effectively during periods of hot weather. Such dispersal may be infrequent, but once every fifty years for instance, could facilitate colonisation of a new site, provided the habitat is suitable. Entomologists have meticulously compiled species lists for contemporary sites, and have produced lists for sites in the prehistoric landscape. These are powerful tools in assessing park landscapes, though palaeo-ecological information is limited by the preservation of suitable remains for analysis. Invertebrate taxa associated with veteran or over-mature trees in lowland England include beetles (Coleoptera), flies (Diptera), spiders (Aranaea), and pseudoscorpions (Pseudoscorpiones), with species dependant on specific stages of decaying wood or bark, and particular humidities and temperatures. Not all the taxa are specific to old trees, some such as the furniture beetle (*Anobium*), the larvae of which are the woodworm, have adapted to old buildings, and even seasoned timber in the open air. A few species such as the highly synanthropic death-watch beetle (*Xestobium rufovillosum*) have their only records away from old buildings, in the timbers of ancient park trees (Buckland 1975, 1979). Harding and Rose (1986) provided a very useful overview and, although lists have since been updated, the principles remain very useful. They presented taxa in three categories:

Group 1: Species known to have occurred in recent times only in areas believed to be ancient woodland, mainly pasture-woodland.

Group 2: Species which occur mainly in areas believed to be ancient woodland with abundant dead-wood habitats, but which have been recorded from areas that may not be ancient or for which the locality data are imprecise.

Group 3: Species which occur widely in wooded land, but which are collectively characteristic of ancient woodland with dead-wood habitats.

Harding and Rose noted the dependence of reliable interpretation on understanding species' ecologies, and variation within species' range. Some invertebrates are very reliable indicators of habitat continuity at the periphery of their range, but occur more widely (in hedgerow trees or even gardens) at the core of their distribution. This suggests that with global climate change, some species distributions may vary markedly. The Lesser stag beetle (*Dorcus parallelopipedus*) is locally common in southern England, occurring widely in ash woods and hedgerows, but much more restricted further north. Another species, *Hylecoetus dermestoides*, is widespread in the north and midlands of England, in woodlands and plantations, but much more tightly defined in the south, restricted to a few ancient pasture-woodlands. The most dramatic clusters of records occur at famous sites such as Moccas Park, Sherwood Forest, and Windsor Park, but there are many records for a range of taxa outside known parkland sites (Harding & Wall, 2000). This begs the question of whether some of these records relate to unrecognised remnants of medieval park landscapes and highlights the need for further integrated studies.

The Demise of the Park and the Impact of Landscaped Parks

Rackham (1986) stated that parks were troublesome, precarious enterprises. The boundary in particular was expensive to maintain, especially for large parks. Owners were often absent for much or all of the year, a situation that could lead to mismanagement and neglect. Deer often died of starvation or of other rather vague causes such as 'Garget', 'Wyppes', and 'Rot'. In Henry III's deer park at Havering, Essex, in 1251 the bailiff was instructed 'to remove the bodies of dead beasts and swine which are rotting in the park' (Rackham, 1978). Even well run parks faced ongoing problems of maintenance. Rackham (1986) noted that many smaller parks were short-lived, and by the thirteenth century, some were already out of use. Sometimes a park was retained but its location changed within the manor, with consequent impacts on their delicate ecologies.

During the sixteenth century, the primary function of the park shifted from game preserve and source of wood and timber, to setting of the country house. A disused park might revert to woodland through neglect or deliberate re-planting. Many former parks became farmland, some like Trelowarren in Cornwall, retaining the park pale, bounding the newly enclosed fields. The late seventeenth and early eighteenth centuries witnessed a fashion to impose formal design and rigid regularity on both existing and new parks. Straight, tree-lined avenues, walks, and straight canals dominated landscapes. At the same time, there came a renewed interest in planting trees, and with wide vistas cut through existing woodlands, new woods were designed in regular patterns within the overall vision. Nature was perceived to be under strict control, and the parks paralleled the great gardens and houses they accompanied (Lasdun, 1992).

Changed fashions provided a new lease of life for some old landscapes, however, with the injection of capital necessary to maintain them against pressure to 'improve' *per se*. If changes allowed habitat-continuity, then some original ecology such as rare dead wood insects might hang on. As Rackham (1986) pointed out, new parklands were not created from a blank canvas, designers of parks and gardens generally adapted and imposed on earlier landscapes. This could mean working with and maintaining elements of an original park. It might also lead to the creation of a new park that incorporated earlier features from a non-park landscape. Even when formality was very much in vogue it was still felt that venerable trees added dignity to the feel of a country residence. In a social landscape, where lineage and continuity were highly valued, then a park that was new but looked and felt old, made an important statement. The designer would therefore not only plant anew but would incorporate elements of ancient countryside into their new landscapes. Old pollards and other trees from ancient hedgerows, lanes, or other boundaries were retained and made significant in new settings. This ensured that ancient pollards and sometimes coppice stools can now be found embedded in a landscape dominated by seventeenth- and eighteenth-century plantings.

Rackham described these as 'pseudo-medieval' parks suggesting this phase of landscape history both preserved some ancient parks, and created these new sites. He notes the New Park at Long Melford Hall, Suffolk incorporating earlier field boundary trees, similar to the situation in the eighteenth-century landscape park at Chatsworth, Derbyshire. At Chatsworth in Derbyshire, the eighteenth landscape park includes trackways, boundaries, ridge-and-furrow fields, and veteran trees from the old field system. Oakes Park, formerly in North Derbyshire, shows a similar use of old field boundary trees to lend an air of elegance and antiquity to a created eighteenth century park landscape. Such sites can be identified not only from archives and records, but also from field archaeology and from their ecology. Landscape archaeology may include early but non-park features. They lack some ancient deer park indicators discussed previously, but can hold species of medieval woodlands, of hedgerows, and perhaps of veteran pollard trees. Again, this gives a site what I describe as '*acquired antiquity*'. In other words, the landscape has elements that would normally be associated with a genuinely ancient feature or area, but which it has acquired or 'borrowed' from fragments of an earlier period incorporated into a later design. Sheringham Park in Norfolk is a wonderful example of this, with veteran trees and ancient banks, not of a medieval park, but absorbed from commonland when the owner imparked the area in the 1700s. In many ways, this presumably is what the designers hoped to achieve, though perhaps not at the ecological level.

Wooded Landscapes, Forestry and Gardening

Perlin (1989) gives a detailed insight into the issues and demands for wood as fuel and for other purposes, and its impacts on societies over the centuries. A consequence of the over-use and exhaustion of a particular fuel, or of the restricted access for social or political reasons, was the need to find alternatives and sometimes to use less suitable materials. In some cases, the competition or restriction on use was due to the interactions of differing and alternative demands – timber for the navy, versus wood for charcoal driven iron smelting. Both of these competed with the use of wood for fuel – for rich and for poor, but especially the latter. Competition between commoner and peasant and the lord of the manor and between industrial use and domestic have been critical in determining the use of the woods and other natural resources. Hayman (2003) describes eighteenth century British landowners tightening their control over the landscape, with legislation passed to restrict the customary rights of forest communities to harvest underwood. This was a contest between the communal resource and the private domain, the *Black Act* of 1723 restricting woodland access. This affected not only fuel use but also the essential felling of estate timber by tenants for building. Some concessions were sought, such as the supervised access of the poor on one day per month to gather deadwood for fuel from the Sheringham Estate in Norfolk. The latter was an imposed grand park that took a swathe of productive common and farmland for its establishment.

As discussed, the relationship between people and nature, politics and fashion were important in determining the lineage and evolution of park landscapes over time.

Nature and landscape were becoming the concern of the cultured British, philosophers, poets, writers, and artists. The eighteenth century brought a revolution in parkland design with, at the highest social level, symmetry, and orderliness displaced by informality and naturalness. This was the era of the great landscaped park, characterised by large areas of rolling grassland. Some were substantially re-contoured, with naturally shaped woods, clumps of trees (and roundels), individual large trees, and expanses of water. Such natural looking, but mostly artificially created, landscapes had necessary buildings such as lodges and boathouses, and features such as temples, obelisks, mausoleums. From the 1700s onwards, new plants (species and varieties), particularly new tree species were imported and used, beginning a distinctive phase of the ecology of these park. Still with us today are the exotics and in some cases invasive *Rhododendron ponticum*, Giant Hogweed, Japanese Knotweed, and many others.

The designers of these landscapes became both rich and famous, and they left an indelible imprint on the remaining medieval parks. Lancelot 'Capability' Brown (1716-83) left a dramatic legacy of designed landscapes, especially parkland. Key features were the serpentine, grouping or dotting of trees, irregularity, and gentle landscape undulations. Water was manipulated through lakes, pools and canals or rivers, and partly wooded banks. Strategic clumps of trees, and isolated specimen trees carried the eye and mind into the distance. Winding ribbons of trees around the periphery of the park implied continuity (and ownership beyond), cleverly blotting out undesirable views. Brown's landscapes are typically impressive vistas viewed almost uninterrupted from the main rooms of the great house. He generally used long-established and native trees, plus and for special effect Cedar of Lebanon. However, Brown and many of his successors were great destroyers of what went before, with implications for the survival of continuity of former parks subjected to his designs. From this period, we know of great avenues of lime and elm destroyed, as were

formal gardens, but there was little written about the earlier landscape elements that were lost. Sometimes old trees and other features were saved, but much was removed, and not everyone appreciated Brown's work. Sir William Chambers for example described his landscapes as resembling: '*...a large green field, scattered over with a few straggling trees ... (where) he finds a little serpentine path, twining in regular S's along which he meanders, roasted by the sun, so that he resolves to see no more, but vain resolution! There is but one path; he must either drag on to the end, or return back by the tedious way he came.*' The Brown-style landscape superficially may have resembled an ancient deer park, but it was a synthetic landscape designed to please with simplified ecology. Many, if not all, of the productive features described earlier were swept away. These are significantly mown lawn and neatly trimmed trees. In the centre of this is sited the Mansion - isolated in time and in space and with views from within across the vistas without. When we see this landscape with its grazing deer and livestock, it may superficially resemble our image of an ancient medieval deer park. Lanhydrock in Cornwall is a magnificent example of this approach with a large park and massive boundary walls. Nevertheless, this is a synthetic landscape of the 1600s designed to please, and with a simplified ecology. It was disparked by around 1780 but is maintained as a grand landscape (Pett, 1998). The old parks were working landscapes with significant and complex elements of the semi-natural. Parks such as Lanhydrock have ancient and veteran trees, and it is important for both interpretation and management, to recognise their origins and therefore their distinctive forms from the wider working landscape and not from a park as such.

The Picturesque

Brown's successor Humphrey Repton (1752-1818), acquired Brown's reputation as 'an improver of landscapes'. He was less brilliant in water management than Brown, but imaginative with cattle grazing under mature clumps of trees, dotted individual trees, and a surrounding belt of woodland. Along with those of Brown, it is these landscape parks with which most people are familiar. Brown designed his landscapes to be seen *from* the House; Repton made his as settings for the House and those passing by, or approaching. They were intended to show the correct social status and wealth of the owner. This also included advice against improvement for mere financial gain, rather than measured statements in the landscape of status. In *Theory and Practice of Landscape Gardening* (1816) Repton used two views of a recently improved estate, and agued against improvement merely for profit suggesting sympathy for the past and its landscapes. Perhaps in his landscapes there was a chance for continuity and for survival:

'*By cutting down the timber and getting an act to enclose the common, he had doubled all the rents. The old mossy and ivy-covered pale was replaced by a new and lofty close paling; not to confine the deer, but to exclude mankind, and to protect a miserable narrow belt of firs and Lombardy poplars: the bench was gone, the ladder-stile was changed to a caution about man-traps and spring-guns, and a notice that the footpath was stopped by order of the commissioners. As I read the board, the old man said 'It is very true, and I am forced to walk a mile further round every night after a hard day's work*".

It is perhaps to the emergence of the *Picturesque Movement* that we owe the survival of so many great trees. Recognition of the picturesque was important for the survival of elements of antiquity, and ecological continuity from medieval parks. Sir Uvedale Price (1747-1829) wrote of landscapes in a way that reflected the past but looked to the future. The picturesque was less obvious, less generally attractive, and had been neglected and despised by professional improvers. He suggested planting exotics in remote parts of landscaped grounds. '*There seems to be no reason against the familiarising our eyes to a mixture of the most beautiful exotics where the climate will suit them.*' He promoted the leaving of fine old trees, and the making of new plantations, to give an effect of natural vigour.' ...*the rugged old oak, or knotty wyche elm, ... are picturesque; nor is it necessary that they be of great bulk; it is sufficient that they are rough, mossy, with a character of age, and with sudden variations in their forms. The limbs of huge trees, shattered by lightning or tempestuous winds, are in the highest degree picturesque; but whatever is caused by those dreaded powers or destruction, must always have a tincture of the sublime*' (Hayman, 2003). This advocacy of exotics was passed down to Victorian gardeners and now is a matter of concern for many conservationists.

The Victorian Landscapers

By the time of Victorian gardeners and municipal parks, many ancient parks were faded memories or fragments of ecology and landscape. Sometimes swamped by urban sprawl, or agricultural improvements, some survived in whole or in part, incorporated into the final great phase of parkland creation. Sir Joseph Paxton (1801-1865) was one of the major figures famed for Crystal Palace and Chatsworth. Generally considered the finest of the Victorian group, his most beneficial and permanent influence was on public parks and their planting as boundaries between parks and gardens blurred (Lasdun, 1992). William Robinson (1838-1935) was hugely influential with his publications such as *The Wild Garden* (1870) and numerous books advocating the *Gardenesque Style*. He emphasised the strong use of '*wild*', naturalised, exotic species. A pioneer of what are now local authority parks, he generally held to have had a positive influence on landscape design. One of his main legacies to park ecology was his advocacy of naturalised exotic herbs, shrubs, and trees alongside natives, in 'wild' landscapes. These are often amongst the most striking features of parklands today, imposed and imposing on earlier palimpsests. The Victorians continued the process of subsuming older parks and creating new features. These might be in a grand rural setting, or in the suburbs of expanding urban centres such as London, Manchester, Birmingham, or Sheffield. Even into the core of a modern city such as Sheffield, it is possible to find elements of the earlier park heritage or ecology, surviving through all these changes to the twenty-first century. These became important components of many great public parks of the later Victorian period and through into the twentieth century. By the late 1900s with local authority funding decimated by central government cuts, these same parks were easy targets for the budget minders. The recognition that this was massive mistake and a hugely false economy was growing by the 1990s, and there has been a significant move to rejuvenate the urban parks. However, the unique ancient elements are often now sadly overlooked, unrecognised and neglected to the point of terminal decline.

Conclusions: the Decline, Fall, and Re-emergence in the Twentieth Century

The question is then what became of the thousands of medieval parks, large and small, that dotted the landscape. For some there are tantalising glimpses of their fate. Ecclesall Woods in Sheffield is the region's premier conservation woodland today. However, its origins are as a medieval hunting park, for in 1317, Robert de Ecclesall was granted a licence to impark, and this is reflected in modern place names such as Parkhead, Warren Wood, Park Field, and Old Park (Hart, 1993). An overview of the issues of interpretation of the landscape here are presented by Rotherham & Ardron (2006). As noted by Hart (1993) there is further evidence of the use of the Woods for hunting, with a set of depositions taken on October 2nd 1587. These were from George Sixth Earl of Shrewsbury. He stated that he, his father and his grandfather '*used sett and placed Crosbowes for to Kyll the Deare in Ecclesall Afforesaied and to hunte at all tymes when it so pleased them there.*' Thomas Creswick noted that ' ………*ye said Erle George grandfather to ye said now Erle of Shrewsbury hath sett Netts & long bowes to kill deare in Ecclesall and hunted dyvers tymes there and he thinketh that ye said Erle ffrancis father to ye Erle that now is did the lyke.*' Richard Roberts confirmed that '…..*he hath sene the lord ffrancis hunting in Ecclesall byerlow and that said lords officers*

sett decoers there at such places as they thought convenyent.' (Hart, 1993). In the early 1700s, there were also livestock pastured in the woods with horses, mares, foals, cows, heifers, calves, and steers recorded. Gelly's map of 1725 shows a 'laund' in the centre of the Woods and this was planted up in 1752 (Jones & Walker, 1997). In the 1587 deposition (Hart, 1993), it is also clear that wood and underwood are also being taken, and it was this use that was to dominate the former deer park for the next few centuries. It seems perhaps that the hunting use is falling from fashion by the late 1500s, with references to deer hunts certainly from the late 1400s and early 1500s. Was this the reason for the deposition? Excitingly, in the late 1990s, Paul Ardron, working with the author, located the western boundary bank of the medieval park (Rotherham & Ardron, 2001). Here we have some insight into the evolution of a wooded landscape, for which the medieval imparkation was probably the critical moment in it becoming woodland today.

By the late nineteenth and early twentieth centuries many houses, parks, and gardens were subject to neglect or became financial liabilities. In the 1950s, even famous and now highly valued locations like Chatsworth Park in Derbyshire were seriously considered for demolition. Many smaller houses and their parks have long since gone. Other imposed parks on farming landscapes, such as Oakes Park at Norton (formerly North Derbyshire), are now amongst the richest ecological sites in their region. However, despite the well documented conservation value, they lie uncared for and neglected, a social misfit in the landscape of urban sprawl. The losses and severance of the landscape lineage is beyond calculation, and the more so for genuinely medieval parks. The loss of Ongar Great Park, Essex, and a pre-Conquest survival was possibly the worst loss of a visible Anglo-Saxon antiquity in the twentieth century (Rackham, 1986). So what have we left? The nineteenth-century clergyman and diarist, the Revd Francis Kilvert gives some idea, describing the ancient oaks of Moccas Park, Herefordshire:

'........*grey, gnarled, low-browed, knock-kneed, bowed, bent, huge, strange, long-armed, deformed, hunchbacked, misshapen, oakmen with both feet in the grave yet tiring down and seeing out generation after generation.*'

Parks and great trees may '*survive*' in new landscapes, housing or agriculture, but most are erased from land and memory. Even if the trees survive, there is no means to replace them as time and nature run their course; so the remaining sites are conservation icons, often isolated in time and space. They possess a unique resource of ecology: lichens, bryophytes, insects, spiders and more, enmeshed with a cultural lineage from the great forests of northwestern Europe.

How we find, preserve, and conserve this heritage is a huge challenge. There is no single approach and correct answer. Involving local people and engaging with local communities must be a key. There is a further issue too. It is now suggested and accepted, at least in part, that remnants of medieval parks are vestiges of very ancient landscapes; albeit transformed and manipulated by human hand over the centuries. These may precede human domination and agriculture, with Vera's vision of forested savannah indicates a lineage to great primeval origins of the European forest. Harking back evocatively to the past, this view also informs the future. The vision of landscapes is freed from anthropogenic constraints of medieval agricultural and pastoral scenes, setting new challenges for deeply embedded precepts of nature conservation. The best working examples are in the remains of once numerous and great, medieval parks, a powerful lineage. Individual case studies prove hugely rewarding and informative and the recent seminal volume on the Duffield Frith in Derbyshire (Wiltshire *et al*., 2005) is a wonderful example of what can be achieved.

For the wider public, their gaze is often upon a landscape that is not what it seems. The apparently ancient such as much of Chatsworth, is in reality an eighteenth century imposition. The twentieth century public park of Graves

Park in Sheffield is really Norton Park, and an eighteenth century grand landscape embellished by deer, but overlaid onto a medieval deer park with early ponds and other features. Much of this is unrecognised, with maybe more than a thousand years of history and historical ecology locked into this landscape palimpsest. It seems sad that such a major and rich resource is so misunderstood and there is little to engage or to inform the visiting public. If we are to unlock the imaginations and the financial resources to safeguard and conserve these unique blends of heritage and ecology, then it is necessary to engage a wider public and to relate their everyday experiences of say Graves Park in Sheffield, to Moccas or Windsor Great Park at a national scale. I fear that we are still a long way off.

References

Beswick, P. & Rotherham, I.D. (Eds.) (1993) Ancient Woodlands – their archaeology and ecology - a coincidence of interest, *Landscape Archaeology and Ecology*, **1**

Bettey, J.H. (1993) *Estates and the English Countryside*. Batsford, London

Blüchel, K.G. (1997) *Game and Hunting*. Könemann Verlagsgesellschaft mbH, Cologne

Buckland, P.C. (1975) Synanthropy and the death-watch; a discussion. *Naturalist*, **100**, 37-42

Buckland, P.C. (1979) *Thorne Moors: a palaeoecological study of a Bronze Age site*. Occasional Publication No. 8) Department of Geography, University of Birmingham, Birmingham

Cantor, L.M. & Hatherly, J. (1979) The Medieval Parks of England. *Geography* **64**, 71-85

Cummins, J. (1988) *The Hound and the Hawk.* Weidenfeld & Nicholson, London

Fagan, B. (2006) *Fish on Friday. Feasting, Fasting and the Discovery of the New World.* Basic Books, New York

Fowler, J. (2002) *Landscapes and Lives. The Scottish Forest through the ages*, Canongate Books, Edinburgh

Harding, P. T. and Rose, F. (1986) *Pasture-Woodlands in Lowland Britain – A review of their importance for wildlife conservation*, Institute of Terrestrial Ecology, Monks Wood Experimental Station, Huntingdon

Harding, P. T. and Wall, T. (Eds.) (2000) *Moccas: an English deer park*, English Nature. Peterborough

Hart, C.R. (1993) The Ancient Woodland of Ecclesall Woods, Sheffield. Proceedings of the National Conference on Ancient Woodlands: their archaeology and ecology - a coincidence of interest, Sheffield 1992. Beswick, P. & Rotherham, I. D. (Eds.), *Landscape Archaeology and Ecology*, **1**, 49-66

Hayman, R. (2003) *Trees. Woodlands and Western Civilization*, Hambledon and London, London

Henderson, A. (1997) From coney to rabbit: the story of a managed coloniser. *The Naturalist*, **122**, 101-121

James, P.W., Hawksworth, D.L. & Rose, F. (1977) *Lichen communities in the British Isles: a preliminary conspectus.* In: Seaward, M. R. D. (Ed.) *Lichen ecology*. Academic Press, London, 295-413

Jones, M. (1996) Deer in South Yorkshire an historical perspective in Deer or the New Woodlands? Jones, M., Rotherham, I. D. & McCarthy, A. J. (Eds.).*The Journal of Practical Ecology and Conservation Special Publication*, **No. 1**, pp. 11-26

Jones, J. and Jones, M. (2005) *Historic Parks and Gardens in and around South Yorkshire. Wharncliffe Books, Barnsley*

Jones, M., Rotherham, I. D. and McCarthy, A. J. eds. (1996) Deer or the New Woodlands? *The Journal of Practical Ecology and Conservation, Special Publication*, **No. 1**

Jones, M. & Walker, P. (1997) From coppice-with-standards to high forest: the management of Ecclesall Woods 1715-1901. In: Rotherham, I. D. and Jones, M. (Eds.) The Natural History of Ecclesall Woods, **Pt 1**. *Peak District Journal of Natural History and Archaeology Special Publication*, **No. 1**, 11-20

Kirby, K. J. & Drake, C. M. (Eds.) (1993) Dead wood matters: the ecology and conservation of saproxylic invertebrates in Britain. *English Nature Science*, 7, English Nature, Peterborough

Langton, J. & Jones, G. (Eds.) (2005) *Forests and Chases of England and Wales c.1500-c.1850. Towards a survey & analysis.* St John's College Research Centre, Oxford

Lasdun, S. (1992) *The English Park: Royal, Private and Public.* The Vendome Press, New York

Liddiard, R. (2003) The deer parks of Domesday Book. *Landscapes*, **4** (1) 4-23

Mileson, S.A. (2005) The importance of parks in fifteenth-century society. In: Clark, L. (Ed.).*The Fifteenth Century V.* Boydell and Brewer, Woodbridge, 19-37

Muir, R. (2005) *Ancient Trees Living Landscapes.* Tempus, Stroud.

Neave, D. and Turnbull, D. (1992) *Landscaped Parks and Gardens of East Yorkshire.* Georgian Society for East Yorkshire, Bridlington.

Perlin, J. (1989) *A Forest Journey.* Harvard University Press, Massachusetts

Peterken, G.F. (1981) *Woodland Conservation and Management.* Chapman & Hall, London

Peterken, G.F. (1996) *Natural Woodland: Ecology and Conservation in Northern Temperate Regions*. Cambridge University Press, Cambridge

Pett, D.E. (1998) *The Parks and Gardens of Cornwall*. Alison Hodge, Penzance, Cornwall

Pigott, C.D. (1993) The History and Ecology of Ancient Woodlands. *Landscape Archaeology and Ecology*, **1**, 1-11

Rackham, O. (1976) *Trees and Woodland in the British Landscape*, J. M. Dent & Sons Ltd, London.

Rackham, O. (1978) Archaeology and land-use history' in *Epping Forest – the Natural Aspect?* Ed. Corke, D. *Essex Nat., N.S.* **2**, 16-57

Rackham, O. (1980) *Ancient Woodland; its history, vegetation and uses in England*. Arnold, London

Rackham, O. (1986) *The History of the Countryside*. J. M. Dent & Sons Ltd, London

Rackham, O. (2004) Pre-Existing Trees and Woods in Country-House Parks. *Landscapes*, **5** (2) 1-16

Read, H. (1999) *Veteran Trees: A guide to good management*. English Nature, Peterborough

Rollins, J. (2003) *Land Marks: Impressions of England's National Nature Reserves*. English Nature, Peterborough

Rose, F. (1974) *The epiphytes of oak*. In: *The British Oak, its history and natural history*. M. Morris, G. & Perring, F. H. (Eds.). Classey, Faringdon, 250-273

Rose, F. (1976) *Lichenological indicators of age and environmental continuity in woodlands*. In: Brown, D. H., Hawksworth, D. L., and Bailey, R. H. (Eds.) *Lichenology: progress and* problems. Academic Press, London

Rose, F. and James, P.W. (1974) Regional studies on the British lichen flora, 1. The corticolous and lignicolous species of the New Forest, Hampshire, *Lichenologist* **6**, 1-72

Rotherham, I.D. & Ardron, P.A., (Eds.) (2001) *Ecclesall Woods Millenium Archaeology Project*. Sheffield Hallam University, Sheffield

Rotherham, I.D., Ardron, P.A., (2006) The Archaeology of Woodland Landscapes: Issues for Managers based on the Case-study of Sheffield, England and four thousand years of human impact. *Arboricultural Journal*, **29** (4), 229-243

Speight, M. (1989) Saproxylic invertebrates and their conservation, Council of Europe, Strasbourg, *Nature and Environment Series*, **42**

Squires, A.E. & Humphrey, W. (1986) *The Medieval Parks of Charnwood Forest*, Sycamore Press, Melton Mowbray

Taigel, A. & Williamson, T. (1993) *Parks and Gardens*. Batsford, London

Vera, F. (2000) *Grazing Ecology and Forest History*. CABI Publishing, Oxon, UK

Warde, P. (2005) *Woodland Fuel, Demand and Supply*. In: Langton, J. & Jones, G. (Eds.) *Forests and Chases of England and Wales c.1500-c.1850. Towards a survey & analysis*. St John's College Research Centre, Oxford

Whitaker, J. (1892) *A Descriptive List of the Deer-Parks and Paddocks of England*. Ballantyne, Hanson & Co., London

Whitehead, G.K. (1964) *The Deer of Great Britain and Ireland*. Routledge and Kegan Paul Ltd., London

Whitehead, G.K. (1980) Hunting and Stalking Deer in Britain through the Ages. Batsford, London

Williamson, T. (2006) *The Archaeology of Rabbit Warrens*. Shire Publications Ltd., Risborough, Buckinghamshire

Wiltshire, M., Woore, S., Crips, B. & Rich, B. (2005) *Duffield Frith: History & Evolution of the Landscape of a Medieval Derbyshire Forest*, Landmark Publishing Ltd, Ashbourne

Animal bones and animal parks

Naomi Sykes
University of Nottingham

Abstract

Animals have always been central to the creation, use, and perception of cultural landscapes. Physically, the location and form of settlements, roads and enclosures reflect human-animal interactions. In other cases animals may play a more psychological role in the construction of landscapes; their visual, audio and physical qualities providing media through which humans might experience and understand the world around them. Indeed, the meaning of a space is often defined, or at least evoked, by the human-animal interactions performed within it: maintaining domestic cattle within a field, chasing red deer across hunting grounds, or simply hearing the shrieks of seagulls at the coast. Despite this, landscape studies have all too often removed animals from the equation, seeing humans as the only significant agent in landscape construction.

Medieval park studies are prime examples of this over-sight; landscape historians and archaeologists traditionally placing more emphasis on park boundaries than the animals and activities that occurred within the pale (Crawford, 1953; Cantor & Wilson, 1961). More recently, the economic and social functions of parks have started to be recognised, with enclosures described variously as game larders (Birrell, 1992), masculine hunting spaces (Gilchrist, 1999, 145), signifiers of Norman identity (Sykes, 2005), and socially divisive symbols of power (Liddiard, 2000; Herring, 2003). Without giving detailed consideration to the meaning of, and human interaction with, the animals these enclosures contained, however, it seems difficult to elucidate their function and social significance. In the absence of this information it is not possible to know if or how the meaning of wild animal enclosures changed through time; whether, for example, Anglo-Saxon hunting reserves should be viewed in the same way as post-Conquest menageries or later medieval parks.

This paper seeks to put animals back into the landscape. By combining a large zooarchaeological dataset (derived from Sykes (2007)) with evidence from animal behaviour, history, iconography and anthropology, it is hoped that the shifting function and meaning of wild animal enclosures can be clarified. Furthermore, it will be demonstrated that, through scientific analysis of animal remains, imparkment can be detected even where physical evidence of enclosure is archaeologically invisible. This opens a new avenue for considering the ancestry of British parks, providing support for the growing opinion that they should no longer be considered a Norman innovation (Liddiard, 2003).

References

Birrell, J. (1992) Deer and deer farming in medieval England. *Agricultural History Review*, **40 (2)**, 112-26

Cantor, L. M. & Wilson, J. D. (1961) The mediaeval deer-parks of Dorset: I. *Dorset Natural History and Archaeology Society*, **83**, 109-116

Crawford, O.G.S. (1953) *Archaeology in the Field*. Dent, London

Gilchrist, R. (1999) *Gender and Archaeology: Contesting the Past*. Routledge, London

Herring, P. (2003) Cornish medieval deer parks. In: Wilson-North, R. (ed.) *The Lie of the Land: Aspects of the Archaeology and History of the Designed Landscape in the South West of England*, The Mint Press, Exeter, 34 -50

Liddiard, R. (2000) Landscapes of Lordship: The Castle and the Countryside in Medieval Norfolk, 1066-1200. *British Archaeological Reports British Series*, **309**, Oxford

Liddiard, R. (2003) The deer parks of Domesday Book. *Landscape*, **4 (1)**, 4-23

Sykes, N. J. (2005) Hunting for the Normans: zooarchaeological evidence for medieval identity. In: Pluskowski, A. (Ed.) *Just Skin and Bones? New Perspectives on Human-Animal Relations in the Historical Past. British Archaeological Reports, International Series*, **1410** Archeopress, Oxford, 73-80

Sykes, N. J. (2007) *The Norman Conquest: A Zooarchaeological Perspective. British Archaeological Reports, International Series*, **1656,** Aracheopress, Oxford

The National Trust's Historic Parkland Project

David Thackray
Head of Archaeology, National Trust

Introduction

The National Trust owns and manages an exceptional collection of around 180 historic parks, the majority associated with historic houses. Many of these properties were originally medieval hunting parks and they retain survivals of much earlier wood pasture landscapes.

Parks range in size from just a few hectares, providing the setting and landscape context for house and garden, to great designed landscapes. Whatever their size or date, they all share a range of specialist values and significances, often with differing, even conflicting, conservation objectives. This makes their management a real challenge for the Trust.

Developing a common approach

The resolution of the acknowledged differences of opinion, the desire to develop a common approach, which recognises, considers and respects significance, and the delivery of careful, balanced, conservation management, were seen as priorities for the Trust's newly established Conservation Directorate. Therefore, in early 2004, a two-day seminar for staff of the directorate was organised to consider these issues and to work towards an integrated, interdisciplinary solution.

Six important objectives were agreed for the event:

- To increase awareness amongst all disciplines of the multiple interests in, and values of, parkland;

- To develop mutual understanding and respect between those approaching parkland from different perspectives;

- To lay the foundations for a shared vision amongst disciplines regarding the future management of Trust parklands;

- To develop mechanisms for joint working between disciplines on parkland issues and for provision of joined-up advice on parkland management;

- To identify further work needed to reinforce or further develop the objectives above;

- To agree the means of promoting the understanding reached to the wider Trust.

Integrated Management and Definition of Conservation

The National Trust has developed a definition of conservation, which brings into sharp focus the responsibilities required for this outstanding and unique collection of over 180 historic parks; sensitive landscapes of great diversity which are vulnerable to the impacts of adverse change and require careful conservation management. It states:

Conservation is the careful management of change. It is about revealing and sharing the significance of places and ensuring that their special qualities are protected, enhanced, understood and enjoyed by present and future generations.

It is true that the Trust has carried out pioneering work in a range of disciplines within historic parks. These included important landscape and habitat restoration schemes and access initiatives. However, there is a perception that much still remains to be done to raise standards of management. Therefore, our objectives should also seek to develop proper understanding of the significance of parks, to ensure comprehensive management planning, to achieve good standards of conservation for all features of historic parks, and to avoid developments that adversely affect the fabric or special atmosphere of parks.

Integrated conservation and project management will need to embrace a range of interests, including:

- Access for visitors which yields enjoyment and appreciation of a range of social and cultural values;

- The importance of trees, particularly the outstanding survivals of veteran trees;

- Wildlife diversity and habitat management;

- Landscape design and aesthetics, including the role of parks as the setting for important buildings and gardens;

- Archaeology and the historical development of the parkland landscape;

- Historical associations;

- Agriculture, land use and the needs of tenant farmers.

There were three core topics addressed by the seminar.

What do we want from National Trust parklands?

The debate identified the need to research, assess, and understand significance, to identify threats and to protect significance. Appropriate, sustainable conservation management and monitoring is needed to establish and maintain the whole park, its environment, and its component features in appropriate condition. The importance of public benefit was emphasised.

What is preventing us from achieving what we want?

A range of threats was identified. These included the impact of land-use practices, particularly ploughing and the use of chemical pesticides; external environmental, social, and economic influences; the lack of understanding of significance, of integrated guidance and of management needs; poor communication of our objectives; inadequate or ill-defined resources. Perhaps most importantly, a lack of common conservation principles needs to be addressed.

How do we move forward?

This session was very positive and agreed the need for improved knowledge and understanding, for the preparation of a series of guidance notes to improve management and for a group to champion and communicate the issues and principles established.

Historic Parklands Group

Following the seminar, the Conservation Directors agreed to the creation of an *Historic Parklands Group* with the following terms of reference:

- To agree a set of principles for managing parklands for circulation.

- To identify and co-ordinate the production of a series of integrated issue-based guidance notes relating to historic parks.

- To assess threats to historic parks and to consider responses and priorities.

- To communicate all these through publications, workshops and advisory visits.

Outcomes

The Group has now prepared Policy and principles for the management of historic parks, accompanied by a series of technical guidance notes. The paper reviews the approach and case studies to illustrate particular issues.

The wood-pasture theory and the deer park: the grove - the origin of the deer park

Frans Vera

Introduction

A widespread belief that is strongly locked in the mental maps of people is that Europe was once covered with a closed canopy forest wherever trees could grow (Vera, 2000). This is based on the theory that naturally a plant community develops towards so-called the climax vegetation. On places where trees can grow the climax vegetation would have been a closed canopy forest, also mentioned as the wildwood (Rackham, 1980; 2003; Peterken, 1996). This wildwood is used as the frame reference for the interpretation of data in the research of the history of forests, woods as well as deer parks (Rackham, 1980; 2003; Hooke, 1998a, b; Wager, 1998).

During thousands of years Mankind is supposed to have changed the wildwood by grazing livestock. This grazing would have brought about a degeneration of the wildwood by a so-called retrogressive succession from the wildwood to open grassland or open heathland. The park-like, wood-pasture would have been an intermediate phase in this process of degeneration (Ellenberg, 1988; Peterken, 1996). In this theory, livestock and trees are supposed to be incompatible, because the animals prevent the regeneration of trees in the forest (Peterken, 1996; Mountford *et al.*, 1999; Mountford and Peterken, 2003). Therefore livestock are characterised as destroyers of the forest (Landolt, 1866; Krause, 1898; Forbes, 1902; Tansley, 1911; 1953).

Recently, the so-called wood-pasture theory has been put forward by Vera (2000) as an alternative for the wildwood theory. The wood-pasture theory makes clear that livestock and trees are compatible. In this theory, the grazing and browsing by large ungulates like Aurochs, Tarpan, Red Deer, Elk, Roe Deer, Wild Boar and European Bison, are the driving forces

behind a park-like landscape. This consists of a shifting mosaic of open grassland, spiny scrub and solitary trees and groves emerging from spiny scrub. The wood-pasture system is considered as the closest modern analogue of this primeval vegetation. In the wood-pasture system, livestock like cattle and horse prove to have been ecological proxies for their wild ancestors Aurochs and Tarpan (Vera, 2000; Vera *et al.*, 2006). The wood-pasture theory claims to explain how large herbivores like oxen and horses make it possible for light-demanding tree species like Oak can survive together with shade tolerant tree species like Beech, Lime, Hornbeam, Ash, and Elm, as they did for thousands of years in the primeval vegetation. The wildwood theory is rejected because all over Europe, in forest reserves that are considered to be modern analogues of the primeval forest vegetation, and where large ungulates like cattle and horse are removed, oak and other light demanding tree-, shrub- and other plant species disappear. This is because they are ousted by the shade tolerant tree species (Vera, 2000; Vera *et al.*, 2006). Because the wildwood has been rejected, the frame of reference for the interpretation of data in the research of the history of forests, woods as well as deer parks has been rejected. In this paper, it will be shown that the wood-pasture theory offers an alternative explanation for the origin of the deer park and for other aspects that are connected with the history of the landscape.

The wood-pasture

A wood-pasture consists of a mosaic of grassland, thorny shrubs and thorny scrub thickets and groves, that are surrounded by thorny scrub. Contrary to the premise mentioned above, trees regenerate very well in the wood-pastures in the presence of livestock. Livestock facilitates the regeneration of trees there by creating by grassland with short vegetation where so-called nurse species can establish themselves (Vera, 2000; Bakker *et al.*, 2005; Smit *et al.*, 2005; 2006). Nurse species are light demanding plant species that are less palatable or not at all palatable for livestock, and therefore avoided by them. They are avoided because they are armed with thorns or spines, like Sloe (*Prunus spinosa*), Hawthorn (*Crataegus monogyna*) and Juniper (*Juniperus communis*), or contain poisonous chemicals, like the Great Yellow Gentian (*Gentiana lutea*) (Bakker *et al.*, 2004; Smit *et al.*, 2005; 2006). Seedlings of trees that germinate close to or in the direct vicinity of such a shrub or herb are protected by the nurse species protect against grazing, browsing and trampling by the large ungulates (Rousset & Lepart, 1999; Vera, 2000; Vera *et al.*, 2006; Bakker *et al.*, 2004; Smit *et al.*, 2005; 2006). They grow up successfully with densities of livestock and deer that make the regeneration of trees within a forest unthinkable (Vera, 2000). This process is called associational resistance (Olff *et al.*, 1999; Callaway *et al.*, 2000; Milchunas & Noy-Meir, 2002).

The mechanism behind the regeneration of trees in the wood-pasture system provides an alternative theory about the origin of deer parks. In particular, clonally-spreading, spiny species like Sloe play an important role in this new theory. This is because of the particular features that this shrub creates in wood pastures under the influence of grazing livestock. These features are groves.

The development of groves

Groves are known from written sources dating back to the Anglo-Saxon and Old English period. In Anglo-Saxon they are known as *graua, graue, graf* and in Old English as *grava, graf, grove* (Hooke, 1998a; Wager, 1998). A grove is a group trees together in a convex shape that can clearly be distinguished from its surroundings, because it is open grassland (Picture 1). It is mainly Sloe that gives the grove its characteristic convex shape, because this shrub spreads clonally from a nucleus in every direction in open grassland. Tree

Picture 1

seedlings establish themselves in the advancing front of this spiny shrub, which acts as a nurse for the tree seedlings and saplings. In this way the Sloe develops a convex shaped scrub where trees regenerate and advance in the open grassland with the pace of the fringes of the thorny scrub from which they emerge (Watt, 1924; Pott and Hüppe, 1991). In this way the collection of trees that emerges from the scrub acquires the same convex shape as the scrub (Vera, 2000).

As the trees grow high, they spread their crown and a closed canopy is formed. The light-demanding nurse scrub beneath them disappears, because it is killed by the shade. As a result there is no shrub layer inside the grove (Watt, 1934; Putman, 1986; Vera, 2000) (see Picture 2) (Putman, 1986; Vera, 2000; Mountford *et al.*, 1999; Mountford and Peterken, 2003). The Sloe survives by spreading into the grassland ahead of the

Picture 2

advancing front of trees into the grassland. In this way it forms a circular advancing spiny scrub around the grove. The sloe scrub marks the transition of grassland to grove and forms a so-called thorny or spiny mantle and fringe vegetation (Watt, 1924; Ellenberg, 1988; Pott & Hüppe, 1991; Rackham, 2003). Large ungulates that inhabit the wood-pasture are known to enter groves through narrow openings in the spiny scrub (see Picture 3).

When a gap in the canopy of the grove is formed, the establishment of young trees is prevented by the large ungulates. Fungi may facilitate the process of opening up the canopy and the demise of the trees (Green, 1992; Dobson & Crawley, 1994) as well as drought and storms (Mountford & Peterken, 2003). Grasses, whose seeds often are brought in by the large ungulates by means in their dung and on their fur, establish themselves in this way and a lawn is or several lawns are formed within the grove (Putman, 1986; Bokdam, 2003; Mountford & Peterken, 2003). As more trees die, the grove becomes more and more open from the centre onwards and the surface of open grassland increases in proportion. In this way a grove changes gradually from the centre onwards into open grassland (Peterken, 1996; Mountford *et al.*, 1999; Mountford and Peterken, 2003; Bokdam, 2003) (see Picture 4). Some individual old trees may hold for longer, giving the grassland a savannah-like look. Eventually in due time trees will regenerate again in the open grassland by means of nurse species in a way that has been described before.

Picture 4

In this way the large ungulates induce in the wood-pasture system a non-linear succession, namely: grassland à thorny shrubs à grove à grassland à thorny shrub à grove *etc.* This results in a spatially shifting mosaic of grasslands and groves (forests) (Vera, 1997; 2000; Vera *et al.*, 2006; Olff *et al.*, 1999). If the nurse species that protects a young tree does not spread clonally, like Hawthorn and Juniper, a savannah-like landscape will be formed (see Picture 5).

The haga; the mantle and fringe vegetation around the grove as a barrier for animals

The link between the grove in the wood pasture system and the deer park is that the mantle and fringe vegetation that surrounds the grove is an impenetrable barrier for animals. This impenetrability nursed the saplings and young trees and made the regeneration of trees possible in the presence of very high densities of grazing and browsing large ungulates. Written sources show that the spiny mantle and fringe vegetation was used for cutting firewood,

Picture 3

Picture 5

known as coppice (derived from Old French *copeiz*, meaning thicket for cutting) (Wager, 1998; Vera, 2000). What was used as coppice is also known from written sources as *hag* (Rackham, 1993; Gulliver, 1998; Hooke, 1998a). The term would usually have meant a forest with a hedge around it (Rackham, 1980). This indicates that the mantel and fringe vegetation was called a *hag* or *haga*. In medieval charters, the word *haga*, *hag*, *hege*, *haye*, and *haya* also meant boundaries; an impenetrable barrier and line of defence (Hooke, 1998a, b). In the early Middle Ages before William the Conqueror (1066), *hage* or *haga* in charters is also related to catching deer (Rackham, 1980, pp. 188-191). Documents from the tenth and eleventh centuries show that a *haga* was a permanent enclosure into which wild animals were driven through a narrow opening. This was done with deer as well as with wolves and wild boars, as becomes clear by the Germanic terms of *wulf hagan*, *swin hagan*, and *derhage*, (Hooke, 1998b; Rackham, 1980; 2003). From the way a grove develops in a wood pasture system the picture emerges of a grove as a convex shaped feature, encircled (or you might say enclosed) by a spiny mantle and fringe vegetation impenetrable for animals. This picture also clearly emerges from Medieval Dutch texts dating from the thirteenth to the fifteenth century. There *hage* appears very frequently in combination with the word *bosch* (meaning grove) as the phrase *bosch ende haghe* (grove and hedge) (De Haan, 1999; M.J.M. de Haan, Roelofsarendsveen, 2000, pers. comm.). Analogues to the oldest boundaries of coppice wood, all the deer parks have a convex shape that is the characteristic shape of a grove, surrounded by a *haga*. They were generally not so large, namely 40-80 ha, although there were also very large ones (1600 ha) and very small ones (6 ha) (see Rackham, 1975; 1980; 1993; Cantor, 1982; Hooke, 1998a, b).

Conclusion

As can be concluded from all this information, the *haga* or the *hag* was the spiny mantle and fringe vegetation that encircled a grove and formed the transition between open grassland and trees. It acted as a barrier that was impenetrable for animals from the outside and nursed seedlings and saplings of trees. It was also impenetrable from the inside, acting as an enclosure that kept wild enclosed in a relatively small area. The reason that the *haga* was mentioned as such was that it was the functional feature, the barrier that enclosed deer (and formerly also wolves or wild boars) after they were driven through a small opening in the *haga*. After this opening was closed, the animals could be hunted inside the grove surrounded by the *haga*. The grove itself would have been very suitable for hunting. Because a shrub layer was lacking and it will have had an open structure concerning the space between the trees as well as there may have been lawns in the centre, as is known from present-day groves. There would have been good visibility and moving around on horseback would have been possible (see Picture 3). It seems plausible that from a certain moment onwards deer were kept permanently in the *haga* for hunting purposes. In this way the grove in the wood-pasture system would have evolved to the historic deer park. If the *haga* changed into a permanent enclosure, the mantle and fringe vegetation would have to remain closed. Through the years, openings would have appeared in the *haga*, because scrub would have died off. These openings should have to be filled. This could be done by planting dead or living thorny bushes. In time, poles could have been used instead, because they offered more security in terms of exclusion. Between the poles a screen could have been placed. This makes it plausible why such a screen used in deer hunting was also called a *haga* (see Hooke, 1998b). In this way the meaning of *haga* evolved through time from a spiny barrier around a grove in the uncultivated wilderness, or in its closest modern analogue, the wood-pasture system, to the spiny enclosure round the deer park and eventually into a fence made out of poles (see Rackham, 1980; Hooke, 1998a, b). The common denominator through time is that the *haga* was: a barrier impenetrable to animals.

References:

Bakker, E.S., Olff, H., Vandenberghe, C., De Maeyer, K., Smit, R., Gleichman, J.M. & Vera, F.W.M. (2004) Ecological anachronisms in the recruitment of temperate light-demanding tree species in wooded pastures. *Journal of Applied Ecology*, 41, 571-582

Bokdam, J. (2003) *Nature conservation and grazing management. Free-ranging cattle as driving force for cyclic vegetation succession.* PhD Thesis, Wageningen University, Wageningen

Callawy, R.M., Kikvidze, Z. & Kikodze, D. (2000) Facilitation by unpalatable weeds may conserve plant diversity in overgrazed meadows in the Caucasus Mountains. *Oikos*, **89**, 275-282

Cantor, L. (1982) Forests, chases, parks and warrens. In: Cantor, L. (Ed.) *The English Medieval Landscape*. Croom Helm, London, pp. 56-85

Dobson, A. and Crawley, M. (1994) Pathogens and the structure of plant communities. *Trends in Ecology and Evolution*, **9**, 303-398

Ellenberg, H. (1988) *Vegetation Ecology of Central Europe*. 4th Edn. Cambridge University Press, Cambridge

Forbes, A.C. (1902) On the regeneration and formation of woods from seed naturally of artificially sown. *Transactions of the English Arboricultural Society*, **5**, 239-270

Green, T. (1992) The Forgotten Army. *British Wildlife*, **4**, 85-86

Hooke, D. (1998a) *The Landscapes of Anglo-Saxon England. Leicester* University Press, London and Washington

Hooke, D. (1998b) Medieval forests and parks in southern and central England. In: Watkins, C. (Ed.) *European woods and forests. Studies in Cultural History.* CAB International, Wallingford, United Kingdom, 19-32

Krause, E.H.L. (1892a) Die Heide. Beitrag zur Geschichte des Pflanzenwuchses in Nordwesteuropa. *Engleis Botanisches Jahrbuch* **14**, 517-539

Landolt, E. (1866) *Der Wald, seine Verjüngung, Pflege und Benutzung.* Zweizerischen Forstverein, Zürich

Milchunas, D.G. & Noy-Meir, I. (2002) Grazing refuges, external avoidance of herbivory and plant diversity. *Oikos*, **99**, 113-130

Mountford, E.P. & Peterken, G. (2003) Long-term change and implications for the management of wood-pastures: experience over 40 years from Denny Wood, New Forest. *Forestry*, **76**, 19-43

Mountford, E.P., Peterken, G.F., Edwards, P.J. & Manners, J.G. (1999) Long-term change in growth, mortality and regeneration of trees in Denny Wood, an old-growth wood-pasture in the New Forest (UK). *Perspect. Ecol. Evol. Syst.* **2**, 223-272

Ollf, H. Vera, F.W.M. Bokdam, J. Bakker, E.S. Gleichman, J.M. Maeyer, K. de & Smit, R. (1999) Shifting mosaics in grazed woodlands driven by the alternation of plant facilitation and competition. *Plant Biology*, **1**, 127-137

Peterken, G.F. (1996) *Natural Woodland. Ecology and Conservation in Northern Temperate Regions.* Cambridge University Press, Cambridge

Pott, R. & Hüppe, J. (1991) *Die Hudenlandschaften Nordwestdeutschlands.* Westfälisches Museum für Naturkunde, Landschafsverband Westfalen-Lippe. Veröffentlichung der Arbeitsgemeinschaft für Biol.-ökol. Landesforschung, *ABÖL*, nr. 89, Münster

Putman, R.J. (1986) *Grazing in Temperate Ecosystems: Large Herbivores and the Ecology of the New Forest.* Croom Helm, London

Rackham, O. (1975) *Hayley Wood. Its History and Ecology.* Cambridgeshire and Isle of Ely Naturalists' Trust, Cambridge

Rackham, O. (1980) *Ancient Woodland. Its history, vegetation and uses in England.* Edward Arnold, London

Rackham, O. (1993) *The History of the Countryside. The classic history of Britain's landscape, flora and fauna.* J.M. Dent, London

Rackham, O. (2003) *Ancient Woodland. Its history, vegetation and uses in England.* New Edition, Castlepoint Press, Kikcudbrightshire

Smit, C., Béguin, D., Buttler, A. & Müller-Schärer, H. (2005) Safe sites for the tree regeneration in wooded pastures: A case of associational resistance? *Journal of Vegetation Science*, **6**, pp. 209-214

Smit, C., Den Ouden, J. & Müller-Schärer, H. (2006) Unpalatable plants facilitate tree sapling survival in wooded pastures. *Journal of Applied Ecology*, **43**, 305-312

Rousset, O. & Lepart, J. (1999) Shrub facilitation of *Quercus humilis* regeneration in succession on calcareous grasslands. *Journal of Vegetation Science*, **10**, 493-502

Tansley, A.G. (1953) *The British Islands and their Vegetation*. Vol. 1 and 2. 3rd Edn. Cambridge University Press, Cambridge

Vera, F.W.M. (2000) *Grazing Ecology and Forest History*. CABI Publishing, Wallingford.

Vera, F. W.M., Bakker, E..S. & Olff, H. (2006) Large herbivores: missing partners of western European light-demanding tree and shrub species? In: Danell, K., Duncan, P., Bergström, R. & Pastor, J. (Eds.). In: Large Herbivore Ecology, Ecosystem Dynamics and Conservation. *Conservation Biology*, **11**, Cambridge University Press, Cambridge, 203-231

Wager, S.J. (1998) Woods, Wolds and Groves: the woodland of medieval Warwickshire. *British Archaeological Reports*, No. *269*, John and Erica Hedges, Oxford

Watt, A.S. (1924) On the ecology of British beech woods with special reference to their regeneration. Part II. The Development and Structure of Beech Communities on the Sussex Downs. *Journal of Ecology*, **12**, 145-204

Watt, A.S. (1934) The vegetation of the Chiltern Hills with special reference to the beech woods and their seral relationship. Part II. *Journal of Ecology*, **22**, 445-507

Chatsworth: the parkland history

Tom Williamson
University of East Anglia

Abstract

Chatsworth is one of the great designed landscapes of England, incorporating features from every period since the late middle ages. This paper describes an introduction to the history of the park and gardens as a briefing, prior to the afternoon field trip of the Sheffield 2007 Conference. The approach is primarily from a documentary and cartographic perspective. It considers the sixteenth and early seventeenth-century landscape which incorporates the gardens surrounding the great courtyard house (erected by Elizabeth of Hardwick and her husbands), and the great deer park extending along the escarpment to the north and south of the house, and up onto the level moorland shelf above to the east. It also addresses the rabbit warren lying to the west of the river.

The creation of the vast Baroque gardens here in the decades around 1700, and their further development and simplification in the first half of the eighteenth century are briefly considered. The creation of the landscape park, to the west of the River Derwent in the 1760s is examined in some detail.

The subsequent expansion of the park in the course of the nineteenth century, and the destruction of much of the old park are also noted. Chatsworth is an incredibly well documented landscape that was worked on by some of the key designers in England; a landscape from which it is possible to tell the entire story of English garden design. However, more importantly, in the context of this conference, it is a place which allows us to compare and contrast changing ideas of, and attitudes towards, 'parkland' over a long duration.

These issues and the supporting evidence are presented in detail in Barnatt (2005), Barnatt & Williamson (2005), Barnatt & Bannister (in prep.), and Barnatt (this volume)

References

Barnatt, J. (2005) Chatsworth: The transformation of a great estate landscape. In: Rotherham, I.D. (Ed) Crisis and Continuum in the Shaping of Landscape. *Landscape Archaeology and Ecology*, **5**, 5-10.

Barnatt, J & Williamson, T. (2005) *Chatsworth: A Landscape History*. Windgather Press, Macclesfield

Barnatt, J. & Bannister, N. (in prep.) *The Archaeology of a Great Estate: The Chatsworth Landscape*. Windgather Press, Macclesfield

Medieval Parks in Duffield Frith and elsewhere in Derbyshire

Mary Wiltshire and Susan Woore
Duffield Frith Research Group

Abstract

Local people have been aware of the existence in Mid Derbyshire of a forest called Duffield Frith (Figure 1). There have been a few printed articles on the subject regarding the development of this hunting ground associated with the de Ferrers family and later the Duchy of Lancaster. This became a royal forest on the accession of Henry of Bolinbroke to the crown in 1399. Such publications are out of date or fragmentary: there had never been a comprehensive study until 2005 when the book "*Duffield Frith*" was published co-authored by Mary Wiltshire, Susan Woore, Barry Crisp, and Brian Rich.

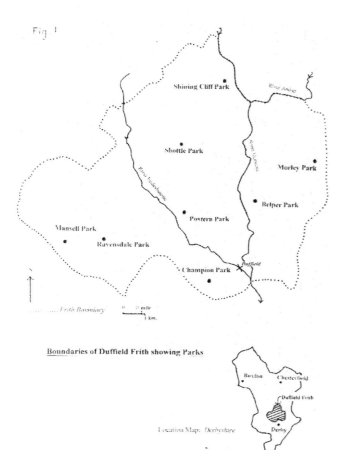

Fig 1

Boundaries of Duffield Frith showing Parks

Figure 1

Part of our contribution involved a detailed study of eight little-known medieval parks in Duffield Frith. This led us to ask whether the features we found here would be replicated elsewhere in Derbyshire and might lead to the discovery of some as yet unrecorded medieval parks.

Following extensive fieldwork, complemented by documentary research, we carefully plotted the bounds of these eight parks and became familiar with their attendant landscape features. From documentary evidence we knew that all the eight parks in Duffield Frith were deer parks and had been in place from around 1300. On the ground the remains of the deer-proof barrier, known as the pale, was frequently found as a degraded bank sometimes up to two metres high with a broad spread. Sometimes this followed present hedge-lines and in other places was a freestanding bank in parkland. The best-preserved stretches of banking were found in undisturbed woodland. In this situation, traces of internal ditches could be seen. Elsewhere in a modern farming setting these had all but vanished. Around the outside of each park a narrow strip of land, a freeboard, marked an extended right of the owner to have access to the pale for repairs and recovery of deer. In some cases this is still referred to locally as the 'bucks leap'. We found breaks in the pale to allow access to the parks, either for people, animals or carts. Several of these have been identified and dependent on their purpose different ways were used for making these breaks in the pale. To allow access to deer and grazing animals, "offset gates" were provided. Here the pale did not follow a straight line but overlapped to provide a funnel in or out of the park as required. On the ground this gives a zigzag. Where present parish boundaries follow the line of the pale there is a kink preserved in the parish boundary where such an entrance is found.

Each park contained at least one lodge. The sites of some lodges have been identified either by place name, documentary or archaeological evidence. Lodges within Duffield Frith were generally used by the parkers, but in one instance a high status hunting lodge with ancillary buildings has been discovered by deep ploughing and confirmed by geophysics. Further investigation is awaited. This particular park has attracted the attention of English Heritage with 88% of the pale, together with the lodge site and the adjacent millpond, being scheduled as a monument.

Certain common characteristics were present in every park: a secure pale, entrances and exits, a freeboard to provide access to the pale, lodges for either parkers or hunting parties and more open areas known as lawns or launds. The latter were clearings or areas without trees and the name survives in field and farm names. There were compartments in some of the larger parks to facilitate the management of stock. There were also enclosed woodlands, holly hags, and alder carrs. From this assemblage of typical park features we found we were able to predict their presence in other medieval park situations.

We are now studying medieval parks in the rest of Derbyshire, building on and revising existing work. As we did in Duffield Frith we are trying to bring together documentary sources and extensive field work to record and map these sites, their possible boundaries, features that still exist and the documentary evidence for them. Where should we look? Old maps showed paled parks, for example Speed's map of 1610. In Derbyshire, there are two collections of William Senior maps from the seventeenth century of the estates of the Cavendish family. More recently in 1981, Clive Hart gave some examples in the *North Derbyshire Archaeological Survey*. In 1983, Leonard Cantor produced a gazetteer and map of medieval parks showing an interesting distribution throughout the county. Most

recently, Gladwin Turbutt published an expanded list in his *'History of Derbyshire'*. Kenneth Cameron's place name evidence is another excellent source. All of these give us obvious places for fieldwork. The landscape features we are looking for are long curving boundaries, border slangs as remnants of the freeboard, bank and ditch earthworks from the pale, offset entrances and anomalies in parish boundaries. The proximity of manorial assets: a mill, fishponds or coney warren/coneygreave are sometimes found in conjunction with a medieval park.

Much recent work by landscape historians on medieval parks has been looking at the possibility that they were the earliest examples of designed landscape. It has become apparent that unlike Duffield Frith not all these parks were deer parks. Our experience is that medieval park owners in Derbyshire were more worried about protecting their assets, (livestock, timber, coal delphs, iron workings) with a secure pale than they were creating an ornamental retreat. This way the owners increased their wealth.

Our working map of medieval parks in Derbyshire is presented in Figure 2. The distribution is much the same as Cantor's 1983 map. Whereas he had identified fifty parks, it seems to us using printed sources plus a great many primary documents and extensive fieldwork, there maybe over a hundred. We suggest that there are some medieval parks unrecorded in current literature. These are now the subject of a structured programme of further research.

Derbyshire Parks in existence sometime between 1200 and 1600

Figure 2